THE
DIGITAL
MARKETING
PLANNER

THE DIGITAL MARKETING PLANNER

Your STEP-BY-STEP GUIDE

With
Annmarie Hanlon

⑤SAGE

Los Angeles | London | New Delhi
Singapore | Washington DC | Melbourne

Los Angeles | London | New Delhi
Singapore | Washington DC | Melbourne

SAGE Publications Ltd
1 Oliver's Yard
55 City Road
London EC1Y 1SP

SAGE Publications Inc.
2455 Teller Road
Thousand Oaks, California 91320

SAGE Publications India Pvt Ltd
B 1/I 1 Mohan Cooperative Industrial Area
Mathura Road
New Delhi 110 044

SAGE Publications Asia-Pacific Pte Ltd
3 Church Street
#10-04 Samsung Hub
Singapore 049483

Editor: Matthew Waters
Content development editor: Martha Cunneen
Assistant editor: Jasleen Kaur
Production editor: Sarah Cooke
Copyeditor: Neil Dowden
Proofreader: Sharon Cawood
Marketing manager: Lucia Sweet
Cover and internal design: Francis Kenney
Typeset by: C&M Digitals (P) Ltd, Chennai, India
Printed in the UK

Library of Congress Control Number: 2021943732

British Library Cataloguing in Publication data

A catalogue record for this book is available from the
British Library

ISBN 9781529742787

At SAGE we take sustainability seriously. Most of our products are printed in the UK using responsibly sourced papers and boards.
When we print overseas we ensure sustainable papers are used as measured by the PREPS grading system.
We undertake an annual audit to monitor our sustainability.

Contents

I need to create a digital marketing plan – HELP!

What does a digital marketing plan look like?

What's the difference between a digital and a traditional marketing plan?

How do I start to create a digital marketing plan?

Answers to these questions and more are waiting for you in this book

1 — 2 — 3 — 4 — 5 — 6 — 7 — 8

Introduction

Creating a plan provides a roadmap to take you from one place to another. Plans ensure that you consider all the items needed on the journey to make the outcome more successful. We know that organisations have been using marketing plans for many years, so what's the difference between a traditional and a digital marketing plan?

I'm using products for goods and services as a term that covers all kinds of merchandise for all types of organisations

A digital marketing plan places the emphasis on the wider digital environment, whether that's via desktop, tablet, mobile, wearable or another connected device. A digital marketing plan pushes companies to consider the opportunities for transacting online, not just promoting their **products** online. It positions digital at the heart of the company.

The Chartered Institute of Marketing defines marketing as: 'The management process which identifies, anticipates, and supplies customer requirements efficiently and profitably' (2009, p. 2), and this process encompasses components known as the marketing mix – the 7Ps (Booms and Bitner, 1980).

All of the 7Ps may be digitally focused or just one (often this is promotion). As to how digital a company can be, this depends on much more than the 7Ps; it's about the organisation, their customer groups and their context.

This is the first digital marketing planner workbook that provides students with a step-by-step guide to creating your own digital marketing plan.

There are eight steps involved in creating a plan and this digital marketing planner will guide you step by step.

There are hints and tips along the way and each step includes the information you need, along with a case example, and then it's your turn to piece together the different elements, apply the tools and create your digital marketing plan.

Throughout the book, you'll see the following icons as useful reminders and signposts:

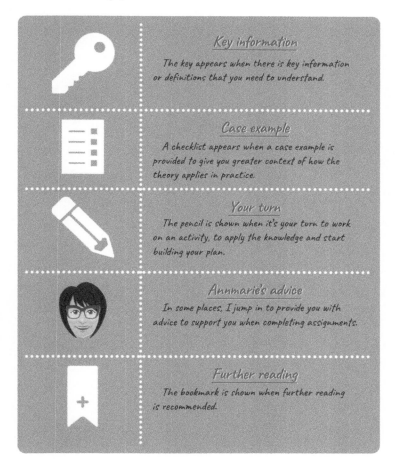

This text is designed as a 'how to' book and is a companion to the main textbook *Digital Marketing: Strategic Planning & Integration* by Annmarie Hanlon. This main textbook contains greater depth and detail, as well as more sources of information, longer cases and examples, if you're keen to explore digital marketing planning further.

The <u>8 Steps</u> in Creating a

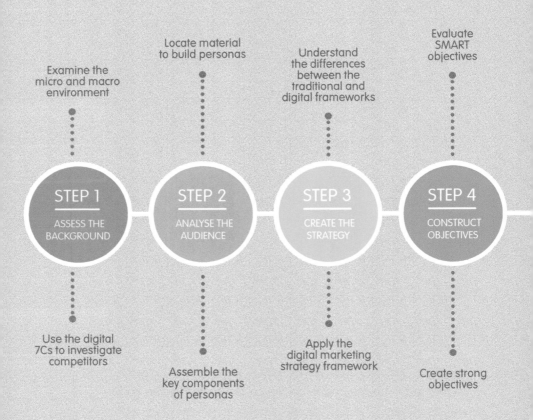

Examine the
micro and macro
environment

Locate material
to build personas

Understand
the differences
between the
traditional and
digital frameworks

Evaluate
SMART
objectives

STEP 1

ASSESS THE
BACKGROUND

STEP 2

ANALYSE THE
AUDIENCE

STEP 3

CREATE THE
STRATEGY

STEP 4

CONSTRUCT
OBJECTIVES

Use the digital
7Cs to investigate
competitors

Assemble the
key components
of personas

Apply the
digital marketing
strategy framework

Create strong
objectives

DIGITAL MARKETING PLAN

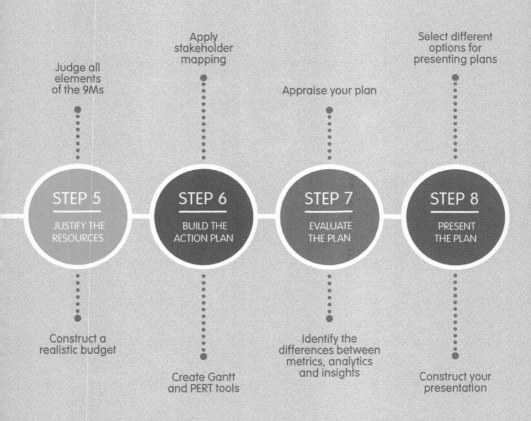

Judge all elements of the 9Ms

Apply stakeholder mapping

Appraise your plan

Select different options for presenting plans

STEP 5
JUSTIFY THE RESOURCES

STEP 6
BUILD THE ACTION PLAN

STEP 7
EVALUATE THE PLAN

STEP 8
PRESENT THE PLAN

Construct a realistic budget

Create Gantt and PERT tools

Identify the differences between metrics, analytics and insights

Construct your presentation

STEP 1

ASSESS THE BACKGROUND

Before venturing on a journey, to make sure you arrive at the destination you need to know where you are starting from. Creating a plan for a company means understanding where they are now, before planning for the future. This is an evaluation of the background and it's more than a simple situation analysis – it's about the organisation's purpose, what's happening in the world and how customers are behaving. It's about contextualising the information and ensuring its relevance to the company at that time.

If you think about how you buy products, there are many steps involved. You may start by searching for something to solve a problem or fulfil a need, comparing different items and evaluating which products meet your needs. So, if you were looking for a new jacket, you might not choose the same website as one your parents would use as it wouldn't feel right and your tastes may be different. You might find different options and explore whether the item suits your budget or can be delivered faster.

When you've weighed up the options, you decide where to place the order. Perhaps you have become aware of a new company and decide to buy from it, or maybe you'll choose an organisation you're familiar with. This is called a **customer journey**.

1.1 Create your customer journey

To create a customer journey, think about an important item you've recently purchased (not your lunch!)

Note here all the actions you took from searching to delivery:
- What words did you use when searching?
- What did you discover?
- Consider what factors influenced your final purchase decision

You may return to this as you work through your plan as you discover which steps you were taking in an organisation's digital marketing plan.

Make notes here:

If you need more room, use the notes section or Scribble Space at the back of the book!

When assessing the company background, you need to examine different pieces of information (we can call this 'data') then you need to analyse the differences and make comparisons or benchmarks. From this, you should synthesise the different data and assess its worth. This enables management teams to make informed decisions – choices based on evidence.

Comparisons in digital marketing are often known as benchmarks*; you take a specific metric and compare*

Key elements in the background to consider include:

- Company conditions (the organisation)

- Competitors

- Context

- Customers – we'll look at this in STEP 2

Let's look at an example of how to evaluate the background of an organisation. The example I'm using is Zoom Video Communications, Inc. (that's the full name and I'll now refer to the company as Zoom), a popular online meeting software that is used by both individuals and companies.

1.2 Choose a company for your case example.

This can be somewhere that you're working, or where you'd really like to work, or a company that you admire.

Note the name of the company you've decided on here:

Company conditions

The company conditions explain the background to the organisation; this provides an overview of their circumstances.

You might already be familiar with the chosen company, but others won't be. It's useful to provide a quick summary that includes:

- The company name

- The type and size of company

- Some background information about the company

- The main products offered

- Their level of maturity in digital marketing

- Other relevant information

Zoom case example – company background

Table 1.1 shows an introduction using Zoom as my case example.

The company background is largely descriptive with basic company data to summarise the essential information, and while Zoom has other services I'm focusing on the main two or this would be a very long plan!

Company name	Zoom Video Communications, Inc.
Type and size of company	A B2B and B2C technology company offering a video conferencing system that focuses on the customer experience
	Over 2,000 employees worldwide and turnover in excess of $2 million
Background	The business started in 2011 and in April 2019 the company sold shares and became listed on the Nasdaq stock market. In 2020 there was a dramatic growth in usage, to such an extent that to 'zoom' became the word for organising online meetings
Products offered	Zoom provides two main services: (1) a communications platform for online meetings, (2) conference room services
Level of maturity in digital marketing	Digitally mature as an early adopter of digital marketing as a cloud-based organisation, with all services available online
Other relevant information	The current focus is sectors that have most need for online video communication: education, finance, government and healthcare

Table 1.1 Zoom case example

B2B *is business to business – transacting with other businesses.* **B2C** *is business to consumer – selling direct to consumers*

Other factors may include price, yet in an online setting this can be variable and changed dynamically, based on factors including: where you're located, your online profile, and comparable products you've liked or may be using. Zoom adopts subscription pricing that's similar to its competitors.

Promotion is also a factor and in a digital environment this can change rapidly and is considered at the planning stage in STEP 5.

1.3 Develop the organisation background

It's your turn! Complete this table to develop the organisation background.

Company name	
Type and size	
Background	
Goods offered	
Digital maturity	

Were you able to provide all the information?

Do you have any knowledge gaps? If yes, more research is needed!

Having gained some information about the organisation, we can now consider the context followed by the competitors.

Context

The context is about the situation or space in which the company is operating. It is important that this relates to the selected organisation as, without this, the details could apply to any organisation in any sector.

The context is in two parts – the **micro-environment** and the **macro-environment** – and the key components are shown in Figure 1.1.

Micro-environment

- The organisation
- Staff
- Customers
- Suppliers
- Stakeholders
- Direct competitors

Macro-environment

- External factors
- Indirect competitors

Figure 1.1   Micro- and macro-environment

The micro-environment addresses internal factors which the organisation controls, such as the staff, customers, suppliers and stakeholders. Traditionally, a micro-environment also included direct competitors and the macro-environment addressed indirect or foreign competitors.

However, *in a digital environment, a competitor is a competitor!* For example, Amazon started as a competitor to bookshops such as Barnes & Noble, Waterstones and Blackwell's, but today it's a competitor to Tesco and Walmart, as well as Netflix. For this reason, I've extracted the competitors to consider separately.

'Customers' is also a larger area to consider and so these are examined separately in STEP 2 – ANALYSE THE AUDIENCE.

Let's examine part of the micro-environment first, using the 7Ps.

Micro-environment

We can use the 7Ps (Booms and Bitner, 1980) to explore the organisation, its staff, stakeholders and suppliers, and Table 1.2 applies this to the Zoom case, as compared to WhatsApp as an alternative video-conferencing system that's popular with students.

7Ps element	Zoom	WhatsApp
Place	• Available via the Zoom website with a single sign-on in many organisations • May be blocked in some countries	• Need to download from an app marketplace • May be prohibited in some countries
People	• Over 2,500 staff • Its main stakeholders are its investors • Main suppliers are Amazon Web Services and Microsoft Azure to provide the data storage required for the software, along with recorded videos	• Owned by Facebook, so staff numbers are not known, but Facebook has over 45,000 staff • Main stakeholders are its investors, governments and external communities • Facebook is trying to address diversity in its suppliers by working with smaller as well as larger organisations, and other groups that are less well represented
Processes	• Easy to download, works on desktop and mobile devices	• Easy to download but works on mobile devices only
Physical evidence	• Had to address 'Zoom-bombing' where people hacked into Zoom meetings to disrupt events	• Often have to manage myths about reading private messages
Products	• Primary product is video communications platform using any device but always requires checking before use as the system crashes unless upgrades are downloaded	• Mobile video calling but limited to around eight people; this is likely to grow

Pricing	• Four main plans: the basic plans are free, whilst Pro, Business and United range from £120 to £200 per user per year	• Free at this time, with no adverts, but this may change
Promotion	• Varied range of ads including tips on home schooling during the health pandemic	• Has engaged in political ads to encourage people to vote in several countries

Table 1.2 Using the 7Ps to assess the micro-environment

Having used the 7Ps to assess the micro-environment, comparing Zoom and WhatsApp, we can conclude that the differences are due to the size of company, as WhatsApp is part of a much larger group, and to the stakeholders. The place factor is straightforward as these are digital tools available via downloads, although they may be prohibited or blocked in some countries due to local regulations.

There are similarities in managing privacy issues and WhatsApp has had to manage many fake news stories and report to governments regarding these concerns. This is a threat to both organisations which they take seriously as WhatsApp employs scams project managers to 'measure, detect and remove fraudulent behaviour from the platform' (Join WhatsApp, 2021, p. 1) and Zoom's senior security analyst's responsibility includes monitoring 'forums, social media, and other threat actor activity channels for potential threats' (Zoom Careers, 2021, p. 1).

Both organisations are heavily reliant on cloud data storage systems which is a potential weakness if there are power outages. Facebook has created its own data centres but Zoom uses those of Amazon and Microsoft, which means that it doesn't have to manage the staff running the centres, rather only to manage the supplier relationship.

At this time, WhatsApp is free, but the number of people able to access the call is limited to eight users. Zoom has adopted a freemium pricing model, as this is popular in digital content services (Mäntymäki et al., 2020). This includes a free option which has limited functionality to encourage users to upgrade and select premium membership.

Annmarie's Advice

A table to show the 7Ps is often not enough to gain maximum marks, so you should add more depth that's supported with academic underpinning to justify your arguments – like this section here

Zoom's promotional messages focus on advice and tips for their users. WhatsApp has taken a different approach and has become involved with political adverts by encouraging people to register as voters, or to use their vote. This means that the adverts may need additional approval before running and can be controversial, according to Katharine Dommett (2019), who has examined the use of adverts on social media platforms.

1.4 Apply the 7Ps

Complete the table and use the 7Ps to assess the micro-environment of your organisation. Introduce the table and add a commentary supported by references to justify your claims.

Introduction to the table.....

7Ps Element

Place	
People	
Processes	

Physical evidence	
Products	
Pricing	
Promotion	

Summarise your key findings from the 7Ps here:

Annmarie's Advice

In the summary, don't repeat earlier content from the table, select key areas and enhance with more depth and detail

Macro-environment

The PESTLE framework often addresses the **macro-environment** and is a mnemonic which represents political, economic, sociological, technological, legal and environmental factors, which we'll explore here.

Most countries follow laws created by governing bodies that introduce legal and political factors which can impact on businesses and how they operate online. Some countries have local regulations banning some types of online businesses from advertising their wares to certain sectors.

For example, **Diageo**, the UK drinks company that owns brands such as Guinness, Smirnoff, Baileys and Captain Morgan, can only promote its products to people in the UK who state they are over 18 years old, with a date of birth pop-up window appearing when entering the website. Diageo cannot control where beers and spirits are or are not allowed, or at what ages this is permitted, but needs to be aware of these issues so that the company can manage its online presence and ensure it does not break local laws.

We also need to be aware of the economic factors, within the overall context, which can influence the success of a product. During the health pandemic in 2020, supermarket sales of alcoholic beverages increased as people stayed at home for longer periods of time.

Sociological factors consider whether the products are socially acceptable or not. Diageo has invested in Seedlip, an emerging non-alcoholic brand that would be acceptable in countries where alcohol is not permitted due to local customs or religious beliefs, as well as potentially popular with a growing number of people that do not consume alcohol.

We also need to be aware of economic, technological and environmental matters, which can all create opportunities and threats.

It is important that you move away from the generic situational analysis and, instead of simply repeating every possible law or political factor that might apply to all companies, focus on the *digital* factors that matter to yours.

Let's return to my Zoom example to see how to apply PESTLE in Table 1.3.

PESTLE element	Current situation	What this means
Political	• Needs to meet data privacy laws, protecting customers' data online as there were issues with 'Zoom-bombing' • This was resolved with a security fix	• Competitors will use any hack as a way to discredit the company, so stringent security policies need to be in place, balanced with ease of using the system • The negative impact could be high and there is a need to monitor potential communications and ecommerce legislation in selected locations
Economic	• Zoom uses a freemium model – a free and paid-for version, it's considered as an essential tool, so less likely to be impacted in an economic downturn but paying members might downgrade to the free version	• This may be an opportunity and Zoom could prepare to offer extended contracts for major customers in a crisis • In better times, encourage customers to move to an annual contract
Sociological	• During the 2020–21 COVID-19 pandemic, Zoom was widely adopted in different sectors and by people of all ages and backgrounds	• Whilst it is accepted, this may be a trend rather than a longer-term reality; more research is needed to explore who uses the platform and why
Technological	• A device is needed to access the products, along with internet access	• Explore how much (or little) bandwidth is needed in comparison to other platforms

Legal	• Legislation varies based on location and for Zoom the main factor is the age of those using the services	• Gather the ages of all new and renewing customers to ensure the legislation is followed
	• This is likely to be 18+ as it may be connected with the ability to pay online	
Environmental	• Zoom has data centres in Australia, Canada, China, Europe, India, Japan, Hong Kong, South America and the US	• Over the longer term, the energy impact may be high, with greater bandwidth required, and Zoom may need to reflect on the energy expended and how this can be mitigated
	• Future health pandemics may result in major demand and outages	• Organise a crisis plan to ensure major customers can still access the platform

Table 1.3 PESTLE applied to Zoom

This PESTLE illustrates the differences between the current situation and how this may impact on the company and thus the action that may be needed. There are some notes concerning the impact and whether the item is an opportunity or a threat. To enhance and support these arguments, cite and make reference to annual reports, market research information and statistics datasets.

This is brief, but highlights the implications; what matters is preparing the marketing response to these elements.

Now it's your turn to assess the macro-environment.

1.5 Assess the macro-environment of your organisation

Use this PESTLE table to explore the current situation and what this means for your company

PESTLE element	Current situation	What this means
Political		
Economic		
Sociological		
Technological		
Legal		
Environmental		

If you need more room, use the notes section or Scribble Space at the back of the book!

Annmarie's Advice

For more marks in an assignment, support your responses with academic references to provide evidence for your claims!

Competitors

Competitors are organisations who seek a share-of-wallet – trying to access contributions that your organisation also wants – whether that's a monthly donation, a regular subscription, a one-off payment or your voluntary time. If you have one mobile phone, you may not need a second. The question is: what's the most effective way to assess competitors in a digital environment? Initially, I'm listing key questions and considering the strengths and weaknesses. After this, I use a framework to add greater objectivity and more academic rigour.

Let's consider who the competitors may be.

According to its Annual Report (Zoom, 2020), the competitors for Zoom include: Cisco WebEx, GoToMeeting, Microsoft Teams, Google G Suite and other cloud communications services.

At this time, the company does not consider FaceTime, WhatsApp and WeChat to be competitors; however, as they provide a similar service, they are indirect competitors within the B2C market.

Table 1.4 shows an overview of some of Zoom's direct and indirect competitors. To illustrate why you selected these organisations, you should assess their relative strengths and weaknesses.

Competitor question	Strengths	Weaknesses
Who are our main online competitors?	Teams is easy to use and gained millions of users during a health pandemic	Has limited user functionality if not in the same 'Team' – cannot add or view files
Who are our emerging competitors?	WeChat offers group calling	WeChat does not enable screen sharing
What marketing activities do the emerging competitors undertake differently?	WeChat provides a social media ecosystem with everything in one single app	WeChat marketing is mainly outside Europe and the USA
How might these competitors impact our business?	If WeChat had a desktop system, this could challenge Zoom Teams includes Office 365 and is an 'all-in-one package'	Zoom integrates with many other platforms

Table 1.4 Overview of Zoom's competitors

1.6 Outline the strengths and weaknesses of the main competitors

Fill in this table and make it richer and more detailed by adding more depth – support your arguments with evidence!

Competitor question	Strengths	Weaknesses
Who are our main online competitors?		
Who are our emerging competitors?		
What marketing activities do the emerging competitors undertake differently?		
How might these competitors impact our business?		

The digital 7Cs for competitor evaluation

We can take this assessment further, as using a digital lens to explore specific online factors can be achieved using an adapted version of the 7Cs (Gay et al., 2007; Hanlon, 2022), where the competitor is directly compared with your organisation. Table 1.5 shows the 7Cs applied to both Zoom and one competitor.

You can add more depth to each of the elements in this table; use the headings for separate paragraphs to provide more detail and don't forget to include academic underpinning to support your claims!

Element	My organisation	7. Competitor: GoToMeeting
1. Culture (company statement)	'Delivering happiness'	"It's not just what we do, it's how we go all in"
2. Convenience	Easy to use in a browser, on a mobile or desktop Has a Teams plugin, integrates easily with other applications	Requires a software download
3. Communications	Branded house approach	Part of the 'LogMeIn' family, so a house of brands
4. Consistency	Simple icon to illustrate the brand	Varied imagery that seems inconsistent, using GoTo as another brand
5. Customisation	Customised portal to access the account	Customised portal to access the account
6. Customer journey	Many call-to-action buttons to reduce the journey	Many options for different customers

Table 1.5 The 7Cs applied to Zoom

1.7 Apply the 7Cs

Using this framework, assess the 7Cs against a competitor

Element	My organisation	7. Competitor #A
1. Corporate culture		
2. Convenience		
3. Communications		
4. Consistency		
5. Customisation		
6. Customer journey		

Annmarie's Advice

It's useful to have a framework to evaluate the background, so that no elements are missed. This adds greater objectivity and credibility to the assessment

At this stage, we have examined the micro-environment – these are the elements that the company is close to and that can impact on decision-making. Some of these elements are managed by the company, which they can change and adapt as needed. We have also explored the unknown – the external factors that are collectively called the macro-environment.

Summary

We've reached the end of the evaluation for the digital marketing plan. We have considered the company conditions, the competitors and the context. This step has also introduced some models that you can use. Be aware that it's better to use fewer frameworks with greater detail than to add in too many models with little depth – that's called theory dumping. It shows that you can copy and paste but doesn't demonstrate real understanding.

Your evaluation of the company background should be started by this time. Remember that you can always return and build in more detail as your digital marketing plan journey evolves.

Notes:

_____

_____

_____

_____

_____

_____

_____

_____

_____

_____

_____

_____

STEP 2

ANALYSE
THE AUDIENCE

For much more on personas including research sources, see Digital Marketing: Strategic Planning & Integration by Annmarie Hanlon (SAGE, 2022)

This step is about our audience, which may be clients, donors, volunteers, householders or supporters – we will call them customers, as one collective group.

Our digital material, from websites to emails, online product offers and social media posts, is about communicating with customers. To ensure they understand what we're trying to say, we need to understand *who* they are. To do this, we need some data. In a digital environment, the demographic identifiers may sometimes be less relevant, because products are bought, not because of age or location or the traditional demographic markers, but due to other factors such as access to technology (webographics) or behaviour (psychographics).

For example, Zoom's customers are not connected by age, gender or location, but by a common need to communicate online.

The concept of personas

These digital segments are often known as **personas** – a view of customers that is often informed by people's online behaviour and interests, rather than by the products they buy.

When creating personas, you might first create (a) a persona based on the current target audience and (b) a second that considers the ideal future persona. We'll create a current persona as part of this step.

To build successful and realistic persons, we need to:

Before we considered personas, one way to divide customers was STP – segment, target, position. Read more in Principles of Marketing for a Digital Age by Tracy L. Tuten (SAGE, 2019)

- Gather **data** – sources of webographics and psychographic data

- Incorporate **realistic features** – a realistic name that's usually paired with a photograph

- Tell **the persona story** – all this material crafted into a persona

There are a range of online tools (some free) that we can use to create personas.

2.1 Explore persona tools

Search online for 'tools for persona creation' to find examples of personas and persona tools.

Be aware that the persona tools still need you to add information to work successfully!

Let's consider the potential data sources first.

Data sources for building personas

Sources of webographic and psychographic data start inside the company. If your chosen company is somewhere that you're currently working, you can investigate if there is a customer database management system. If yes, this may include some insights, such as location (if that is a factor in your company), whether the products are for the customer or a gift (check whether the delivery address and recipient are the same) and some demographic data such as names. You may also have the opportunity to conduct online interviews or organise user research to better inform the data.

Other data sources include:

- Company websites
- Investors' websites
- Government and non-governmental organisations' datasets
- Market research reports
- Online data sources
- Social media platforms
- Analytics or insights programs
- Articles in academic journals

Let's look at each of these in turn.

Company websites

If you're not working for your chosen company, you can explore the company website and read 'about us', 'careers', 'press area', or similar sections, to see how the company describes how it works, its benefits and what makes it different. You can also explore compliments and complaints, by searching for 'company name' + 'review' or '#fail', as these will illustrate the elements of service that customers like and dislike – adding richness to the data.

Investors' websites

Companies with shareholders have separate investors' websites which are a treasure trove of data. These websites provide company reports which often share details about the products offered by the company, its strategy, its competitors, its customers and more!

The investors' website area also includes media information; this is the official background to the organisation, its products and its leaders.

2.2 Search online for more on your chosen company

Examine your organisation's careers page and explore whether there is an investors' website by searching for 'company name' + investors.

Note the details of what you discovered on the careers pages or investors' site here:

Market research reports

If you're at university, you may have additional access to specialist market research reports. If not, you might find that industry associations share snippets of their findings.

2.3 Ask the librarian!

Your librarian has had many years of training and they know exactly where to find information as well as how to search. Ask them about research reports that may be free in your library or search your online library for 'help guides' that will direct you to a valuable collection of reports.

Government and non-governmental organisations' datasets

Governments collect data and much of this is shared at an aggregate level – where individuals cannot be identified. These datasets are often free to access, although they may be a year or so out of date.

Government statistics services across Asia, Africa, the Americas, Europe and Australasia are easily found online and contain demographic and psychographic data.

Non-governmental organisations (NGOs) also collect and share data connected to the research projects being conducted. For example, NGO data sources that capture worldwide demographic and psychographic insights are available from the United Nations and the World Bank.

Online data sources

There are a wide range of commercial online data sources to capture webographic information. They generate an income from advertising (with large volumes of people visiting their websites) or as a way to offer limited details, and further data may be chargeable (the freemium model). If you search for 'online data sources' or 'number of people online', you'll see many websites that provide data on internet access and social media usage.

Social media platforms

Social media platforms that offer advertising also provide access to their datasets, providing useful research material into their users and their online behaviour.

Social media posts from customers also provide further insights – what customers like and dislike, the words they use to express themselves publicly, who else they share the opinions with, and their feelings about the brand. The value of content in these posts, whether on brand pages or in online communities, is an area studied by researchers known as netnography (Kozinets, 2002).

2.4 Examine the social media spaces

Look online at your organisation's social media pages. How many fans, followers or subscribers do they have? What types of posts are created? Are comments made by the followers positive or negative?

Analytics or insights programs

Internal data can be gathered from analytics or insights programs. Typically, these are available from sources including:

- Web analytics
- Twitter analytics
- Facebook/Instagram Insights

However, these are only available if you are working at the company or have access to this data – it's not publicly available information.

Analytics reports are quantitative and show data such as:

- The main devices people use to visit the website (desktop, mobile or tablet)
- The top performing content (best and worst pages or posts)

- Where the visitors came from (social media, email newsletter, online searches)

This data can help towards creating the main personas.

While these analytics or insights programs don't show the data of specific users, they enable the marketing team to know more about how customers hear about the company (awareness) and can demonstrate how well the online customer journey is working (consideration to conversion).

Articles from academic journals

Peer-reviewed articles or papers that are based on empirical research can shine a light on specific behaviours and explain why they occur. Journal articles are strong sources of information that support other data and can enhance your persona.

Your module reading list may recommend specific journals to consider. These might include:

- *Journal of Interactive Marketing* – covers many aspects of digital marketing

- *Computers in Human Behavior* – considers how computers change our behaviour

- *Harvard Business Review* – leads on latest business topics

- *Business Horizons* – an easy-to-read journal

Access to these journals and others is often available via your university library.

2.5 Assess the data that's available to you

Having considered many types of data sources in this section, pause and review what's available for you to examine an organisation in more depth.

Summarise here the key data sources for your organisation:

Adding realistic features for personas

Having gathered some data about the persona, you need to make it real. Adding a proper name is better than saying 'Persona A' or 'stressed student' as it's easier to create a plan that's focused on a real person, such as Martha or Matt. If you're looking for suitable names, you can check the names of those commenting positively on social media.

If you think there is an age range for the products, you can search for 'top boys'/girls' names in YEAR' and various baby names' websites will appear, showing the most popular names in that year.

As an example, if you were preparing a new lipstick line for Fenty Beauty, it's unlikely that your persona would be called Gerald or

Annmarie's Advice

Be careful how you use 'free images' as the owner might retain the copyright and if you add them to a commercial website, there may be charges to pay!

Gertrude! The name should be relevant to the customers, rather than being a name that you like.

Once you've added a realistic name, it's a good idea to add a photograph or an image that represents the persona. This will make it easier when you, or others, are creating content – you can look at them and sense-check whether the content sounds acceptable for the persona. Plus, an image brings the persona to life.

2.6 Find free images

Search online *for 'free images to use' and select one that best fits the name*

Crafting the persona story

It's time to gather all the evidence and to bring all this material into the persona. You should now have obtained data to support the development of the demographic, webographic and psychographic elements. You've selected a name and an image. You might now wish to identify more about why they're buying the product – for what purpose? This could be for its essential nature (supermarket hand sanitiser), for the experience (Dior hand sanitiser), for a gift (Neal's Yard organic defence hand spray) or for another purpose. Understanding 'why they buy' is another piece of the persona puzzle and can be garnered from observing online groups.

Do remember that if you're observing and gathering data from a group, you'll need permission to do this and to address any ethical issues. For example, if you're at university and it's part of your thesis, you'll need approval from the ethics board. Many of the people commenting online are not aware that what they're saying may be used for research purposes, so you need to ensure that you do no harm and do not put people at risk.

Annmarie's Advice

As an ethical minimum, you should blur or remove the images and real names if you're sharing online data, in order to protect your subjects

Part of the purpose of creating personas is to ensure that your digital material is relevant to the target audience – your words should echo their words. For example, if you're creating the product description for a new lipstick for Fenty Beauty, you might start with 'Rihanna's inspo'. However, if you're writing for Estée Lauder then it's likely to be more traditional – you'd say 'product details', as 'inspo' might not be understood by the target audience for that brand!

2.7 Find the keywords

Look at the social media posts and identify the frequently used words or phrases, as these may help to make your persona more realistic.

Note here what you've discovered:

Table 2.1 outlines the persona elements for Zoom, highlighting the differences between their B2B and B2C customer groups.

Persona element	Zoom B2B	Zoom B2C
Name	Alex and Fraser	The Jones Family
Demographics	Busy executives needing online video for fast communication with colleagues in different locations Have budget allocation available	Busy family with relatives across the country
Psychographics	Working together online, sharing material, improving communication between offices	Staying in touch with friends and family
Webographics	All devices, all operating systems (Windows, Macs)	Have many devices at home and willing to pay for longer family meetings

Table 2.1 The persona elements for Zoom

2.8 Create a persona for your organisation

Build your first persona using the boxes.

Persona for my case organisation

Name

Demographics

Psychographics

Webographics

Annmarie's Advice

The name should be a person's name, not a generational cohort such as 'millennials' or 'Gen Y'; and to make it realistic, search online for 'top names in 2000' to see what was popular!

Annmarie's Advice

A persona might not just be a single individual; it could include a family group or a commercial buying unit

Summary

You have explored and analysed the audience in more depth and have a blueprint for a persona. This will enable you to create a second or third persona if needed.

If you're working at a company, it's worth involving different departments to develop the personas, from marketing to IT, web development and the sales team – learn how to use stakeholder mapping in **STEP 6** to get others involved.

Once the personas are agreed, it's critical that they are applied and they can be used for:

- Creating content: words, images and video
- Developing the customer journey
- Testing new ideas for products and services

The more people that are involved in the process, the more chance you have that the personas will be used. You'll also better inform all aspects of the digital marketing plan.

Notes:

_____

_____

_____

_____

_____

_____

_____

_____

_____

_____

_____

STEP 3

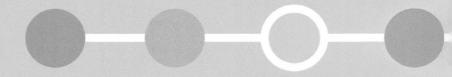

CREATE
A DIGITAL
MARKETING
STRATEGY

Strategy is the step where everyone struggles! Although 'write a strategy' may seem like a major task, in reality a strategy should be short and succinct.

Let's start with what a digital marketing strategy is not! It is not:

- ✖ a list of tactics or actions
- ✖ a set of objectives
- ✖ a note of timed activities
- ✖ a document itemising all content for the next six months

A digital marketing strategy is the **direction for the company** – a statement that clearly states its overall aim and where it is going.

Why organisations need growth strategies

To continue in business, all organisations need growth. Without growth, they disappear; this is because every year some customers may leave as they are provided with alternative opportunities or no longer need the products. For example, you might swap the local takeaway service in favour of the **Just Eat Takeaway.com app** which provides more choice and is easier to use. Or you might only need an online referencing system, such as Endnote or Mendeley, while you're studying and when you leave university you close your account.

Added to this, the external environment plays a critical role and some products may be discontinued or a firm might have to close its business.

For example, **Napster** was an early music-sharing website which, at its peak, had over 24 million users who uploaded their music collections and shared them freely across the network. This meant you'd never need to pay to access music again. But the musicians were losing out on their royalty fees, so initially the rock group Metallica and rapper Dr Dre took legal action against the company. This was soon followed by the major recording companies taking Napster's team to court for copyright infringement, and finally Napster ceased trading.

Other external factors may result in some markets no longer being accessible, such as governments banning social media in various countries (e.g. governments in the USA and Indonesia have tried to block TikTok, whilst those in India and Pakistan have succeeded).

3.1 Examples of companies that lost your custom

Think of a company you used to use but don't anymore and it's lost your custom:

- Why is this?
- Which PESTLE factors may be involved?
- Were there any steps the company could have taken to keep you?
- What do you miss about the company?

Make notes here:

These PESTLE factors are why it's essential to identify those risks. This is a good time to pause and reflect on **STEP 1**, to assess the environment and to double check that it covers all relevant options. An opportunity for one organisation may be a threat to another and this is why most organisations adopt a growth strategy.

3.2 Check the PESTLE details

Return to <u>STEP 1</u> and check to see whether you missed any critical factors.

What were these? Note any issues here...

And don't forget to add these into your assessment!

Having considered why growth is needed, examples of four growth strategies are shown in Table 3.1 with their characteristics, the primary focus and selected digital marketing strategies.

Traditional growth strategy	Characteristics	Focus	Digital marketing strategy
Market penetration	Existing markets/ customers and existing products	Growth from existing customer base using more of the products	Conversion
Market development	New markets/ customers and existing products	Growth from new markets or customer groups	Awareness, consideration, conversion
Product development	Existing markets/ customers and new products	Growth from existing customers buying new products	Awareness, consideration, conversion
Diversification	New markets/ customers and new products	Growth from new markets with new products	Awareness, consideration, conversion

Table 3.1   Example of business growth aims and selected digital marketing strategies

Does this look familiar? If you're studying marketing, it should! Professor Igor Ansoff wrote an article for the *Harvard Business Review* in 1957 called 'Strategies for Diversification' where he commented that 'a business firm must go through continuous growth and change' (Ansoff, 1957, p. 113). You may be more familiar with his work as the 'Ansoff Matrix' which is often used in marketing and management as it is a simple 2 x 2 matrix that considers the main methods of business growth. Table 3.1 also includes digital marketing strategies, which we'll explore next.

Steps in a digital marketing strategy

A digital marketing plan considers promoting and selling products online, so before we can find new customers, they need to be aware of the company. Once there is a level of awareness, we then need the potential customers to consider our offer against others.

Once potential customers are aware and considering whether to subscribe, buy or download, we need them to convert and become customers. Examples of this are being sent an email with a time-limited offer, such as '10 per cent off before midnight!' or 'Subscribe now and gain an extra 20 per cent storage!' These tactics are nudges to encourage the online viewer to make a decision.

This digital marketing strategy framework puts the customer first – working through stages of the customer journey

You might think that this sounds like a long process, yet in an online environment those first three steps could take minutes or seconds!

There is a final step that is missing in the traditional growth strategies – enthusiasm, where we ensure existing customers are happy with the products and ask them to share positive news about the company which contributes to growth. The steps in a digital marketing strategy are shown in Figure 3.1.

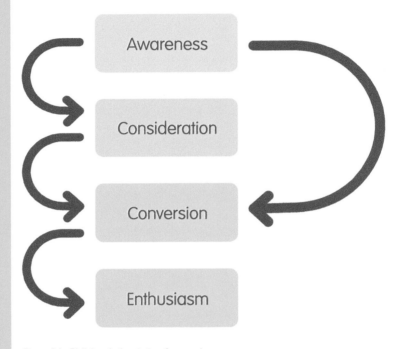

Figure 3.1 Digital marketing strategy framework

In the digital marketing strategy framework, you'll see that the steps are progressive, from one to the next, although in reality there may be forward and backward steps. The final step is enthusiasm, but this might not always be achieved. For example, if you need a laptop stand, you might search online, see an item, add to cart, check out and get delivery the next day – all in less than 10 minutes. If you've bought from Amazon or Alibaba, you may not know the seller as you've made the purchase through the intermediary and so might not bother to leave a review.

The difference between the Ansoff Matrix and the digital marketing strategy framework

The crucial difference between the traditional Ansoff Matrix and the digital marketing strategy framework is that Ansoff is based on action by the organisation, and the digital marketing strategy is based on customer action. It's a reversal of the focus from company to customer. This is a reflection of the loss of control that organisations have in a digital environment as customers can generate awareness much faster than companies can.

For example, during the COVID-19 pandemic we witnessed the growth of TikTok, which had around 1 million daily active users in 2017 and grew to 25 million in 2021. This was less about a market penetration or market growth strategy and more about enthusiasm as happy customers shared with friends, family and colleagues, to such an extent that TikTok challenges were reported on national news programmes.

3.3 Discovering a new company

Think about a company or an app you've discovered recently. How did you hear about it? From friends, social media or in another way?

Application of the digital marketing strategy framework

Let's look at how the digital marketing strategy framework can be applied, using Dropbox, the online data storage system, as an example.

Or you could consider Google Drive or iCloud in the same way, as these systems follow a freemium pricing strategy – limited storage is free, but when you need more space, you have to pay for it.

Table 3.2 shows how the growth strategies are applied and overlaid with the digital marketing strategies, for Dropbox.

You'll see that a key aspect of digital marketing is the conversion action which is present every time.

Traditional growth strategy	Digital marketing strategies			
	Awareness	Consideration	Conversion	Enthusiasm
Market penetration			Encourage existing customers to upgrade	Keep existing customers happy
Market development	Make new customers aware of the company	Encourage new customers to consider Dropbox	Convert new customers	Encourage existing customers to promote the service
Product development	Make existing customers aware of new products	Encourage existing customers to consider new products	Offer existing customers new products	
Diversification	Make new customers aware of new products	Encourage new customers to consider new products	Convert new customers	

Table 3.2 Application of growth and digital marketing strategies for Dropbox

You'll notice that the strategies don't include specific details, or actions or tactics.

So, for diversification, it doesn't describe the new product or where the new market is located. It's a bigger picture decision at this stage. This is because when the details are added, staff often get stuck, trying to figure out who will do this or that, rather than committing to moving into the new market or launching the new product.

Having explored growth and digital marketing strategies, let's see how this works for you.

3.4 Your strategic options

Outline the strategic options in this table for your chosen company. Don't forget, you don't need much detail at this stage, but need to consider where growth will come from, based on your assessment of the company background in STEP 1 and the audience analysis in STEP 2.

Digital marketing strategies

Awareness	Consideration	Conversion	Enthusiasm

Having started to develop your digital marketing strategy, let's return to Zoom as the case example to see how a real business strategy works.

Zoom's annual report follows my earlier comments and clearly states the focus is 'our growth strategy' (Zoom, 2020, p. 4). Having adopted an overarching growth strategy, the company shares its policies to achieve this, as shown in Table 3.3.

Annmarie's Advice

The strategy links back to the earlier steps so that this starts to flow and is connected

Traditional growth strategy	Digital marketing strategy	Policy	Rationale
Market penetration	Awareness to conversion	Expand within existing customers	Move from one department into another within Alex and Fraser's companies
Market penetration	Consideration to conversion	Drive new customer acquisition	Allowing customers to use a free version to become familiar with the subscription system
Market development	Awareness to conversion	Accelerate international expansion	With worldwide customers, expand product adoption to more countries
Product development	Conversion	Innovate our platform continuously	Develop customer-requested features
Market development	Enthusiasm	Keep existing customers happy	Gain referrals from happy Jones Family customers

Table 3.3 Zoom's digital marketing strategy

Using the Zoom example, Table 3.3 highlights the differences between the digital marketing strategy framework and the traditional Ansoff model. Both are focused on growth; the difference is that the digital marketing strategy framework is centred around the online user journey and sees the steps as progressive, rather than simply being about the product or market, as Ansoff did.

Key factors excluded from a strategy

As well as including and referring back to the work conducted in **STEP 1** and **STEP 2**, you'll notice that the strategy excludes some factors:

✖ **There are no lists of tactics or actions**. We don't know *how* the awareness will be gained in wider geographical markets.

✖ **There are no objectives**. This is a statement, not a SMART objective that claims 'to encourage consideration from 350 customers to acquire 100 new customers'.

✖ **There are no timed activities**. The strategies have no dates which means that they could be valid for six months, one year or three years.

✖ **There are no content details itemised**. The strategy focuses on *what* not *how* – that follows later.

You may have spotted a couple of extra columns here too: the policy and the rationale.

Policy is the guiding principle that looks at how the strategy will be achieved, so market penetration and increasing awareness to conversion will be accomplished by expanding within existing customers.

The **rationale** helps to contextualise when building the strategy, but is not included in the actual strategy statement. It's valuable content because it provides the logical approach for how this will happen, again at a top level, without specific details. This is useful and essential in STEP 4 when you are constructing the objectives as the thinking behind this is in place.

The strategy is closely based on the company background that we established in STEP 1 – from the competitors' situation to the context. Zoom maximises competitors' weaknesses; for example, the competitor evaluation noted that Teams had limited user functionality and so Zoom addresses this with a policy to 'innovate our platform continuously'.

The context in STEP 1 highlighted that privacy issues were a concern, which could be used by competitors. To counter this, another policy is 'keeping customers happy', so instead of Zoom trying to convince possible customers that the system is safe and secure, other customers do this for them.

The freemium pricing model is used as a stepping-stone to drive new customer acquisition – both amongst customers and within companies. The data centres in different locations that were noted in the PESTLE model (STEP 1) are applied in the strategy with the policy to 'accelerate international expansion'.

Zoom uses its research to make informed decisions about its strategy. This means that the strategy will be enduring and realistic.

One more issue to consider is that a company strategy may include managing several steps at the same time.

Notes:

_____

_____

_____

_____

_____

_____

_____

_____

_____

_____

_____

_____

_____

_____

_____

_____

_____

_____

_____

3.5 Take the strategy to the next level

You've created a strategy for your company; now add in the rationale as this will help when creating objectives.

You could use the table as a structure for starting the strategy before writing out as a whole paragraph. You can include or remove the Ansoff element if you're more familiar with this – it's up to you.

Traditional growth strategy	Digital marketing strategy	Policy	Rationale

Strategy statement

Having assembled these blocks together, we can create a strategy statement. This strategy statement makes it easier for non-marketing people to understand the overall direction the organisation is taking. Zoom's strategy can be written as:

> *Zoom is adopting a growth strategy which comprises: (1) building awareness within wider geographical markets; (2) encouraging consideration to drive new customer acquisition, leading to conversion; (3) delivering conversion by expanding the numbers of customers within existing companies and adding new product features; and (4) encouraging enthusiasm by gaining referrals from existing happy customers.*

This is a clear strategy that can be understood by the employees and investors alike.

Having seen a strategy being developed and understood what is included – and from where – as well as what is not included, it's over to you to create a strategy for your company.

3.6 Your strategy statement

You've outlined the strategy for your organisation in an earlier action (3.4 Your strategic options) and it's now time to write a summary statement.

This is one or two sentences at most (around 50–75 words) that should summarise the approach, like the Zoom example:

Summary

STEP 3 has explained why growth strategies are essential for organisations. We have looked at examples of business growth aims and selected digital marketing strategies, as well as examining the steps in the digital marketing strategy framework, with examples.

The step concluded with how to create a strategy statement and showed how this works in practice.

You should remember to return to the earlier steps and ensure that each step informs the next, so the plan is connected.

Notes:

_____

_____

_____

_____

_____

_____

_____

_____

_____

_____

_____

_____

_____

_____

_____

_____

_____

_____

_____

STEP 4

CONSTRUCT
THE OBJECTIVES

Strategy considers the direction for a company and the objectives explain what is needed to get there. Objectives focus on *what* not *how*. How objectives are achieved is addressed in **STEP 6**, building the plan.

The strategy (STEP 3) is based on the company background (**STEP 1**) and the personas (STEP 2), and the objectives are then based on that strategy. There needs to be a connection from one step to the next so that the plan works.

Returning to the Zoom example, we'll take one element as an example to show the link between the objectives and the strategy and how the rationale (created in STEP 3) helps to ensure the objectives are connected. Figure 4.1 shows the strategy, policy and rationale and finally one objective is presented.

I've used the enthusiasm strategy and I've referred back to the personas in STEP 2, so there is a thread running from one step to the next.

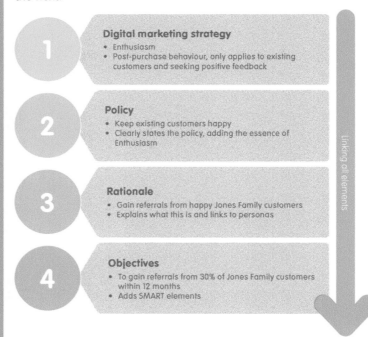

Figure 4.1 The link between Zoom's objectives and strategy

Figure 4.1 provides an overview of how I've created this objective. It may seem like a lot of work but typically organisations don't have dozens of objectives, so it's important to ensure they fit into the overall context and meet the needs of the strategy.

One of the challenges in creating objectives is that sometimes they are developed in isolation, with no connection to the strategy, and this lack of linkage means they will be weak.

4.1 Create an objective

Based on the information you have so far, create one objective for your case organisation. It doesn't need to be perfect, just start writing here …

You've created your first objective and you'll develop further in this step. Using the Zoom case example, let's look at the recommended objectives for Zoom in Table 4.1.

I've removed Ansoff from Table 4.1 so we can see the elements more clearly. This includes the strategy that we considered in STEP 3, the policy underpinning this and the specific rationale that explains and connects this to the company, and finally the objectives. You'll also notice that some strategic options have more than one objective and this is because they are interdependent – connected to each other to meet the requirements of the strategy.

The personas created in STEP 2 are also incorporated into the relevant objectives.

Digital marketing strategy	Policy	Rationale	Objectives
Awareness to conversion	Expand within existing customers	Move from one department to another within Alex and Fraser's companies	1. To convert in-company usage from 20% to 30% within 12 months within Alex and Fraser's companies
Awareness to conversion	Accelerate international expansion	With worldwide customers, expand product adoption to more countries	2. To launch Zoom in India within four months 3. To launch Zoom in Brazil within 12 months 4. To launch Zoom in Peru within 18 months
Conversion	Innovate our platform continuously	Develop customer-requested features	5. To develop 2 new Jones Family-requested product features within 6 months 6. To develop 2 new Alex and Fraser-requested product features within 12 months
Consideration to conversion	Drive new customer acquisition	Allow customers to use a free version to become familiar with the subscription system	7. To convert 20% of Alex and Fraser customers from freemium to paid-for subscriptions within 12 months
Enthusiasm	Keep existing customers happy	Gain referrals from happy Jones Family customers	8. To gain referrals from 30% of Jones Family customers within 12 months

Table 4.1 Zoom's objectives

This table shows that the five policies for Zoom have become eight objectives. Before we examine this in greater detail, it's your turn to refine and develop your objectives.

4.2 Review your objective

In 4.1 you created one objective – does this relate to the earlier strategy? If yes, that's amazing; if no, that's fine, just refine it here, based on the additional knowledge.

You may find the table useful to start the process.

Digital marketing strategy	Policy	Objectives

Having looked at the process involved, from creating the strategy to building the objectives, the next factor is ensuring that the objectives are SMART.

SMART objectives

All objectives should be SMART; if not, they are goals and it's difficult to know when they've been achieved. SMART is a mnemonic that includes five elements: specific, measurable, achievable, realistic and timed.

Figure 4.2 shows how a SMART objective is created, using the Zoom example.

Annmarie's Advice
When you create
an objective,
check that it is
SMART but do
not granulate or
list each element
as this looks
weak!

Figure 4.2 Example of a SMART objective

Let's look at the SMART elements in more depth to see how and where these are covered:

- The need is **specific**: it has one purpose – to gain referrals.

- The objective includes a form of **measurement** – in this case referrals will be sought from 30 per cent of this persona group.

- As the objective is based on earlier research and the development of personas, it is **achievable** and relevant to the company.

- The objective will require some planning and actions before it takes place, so it is **realistic**. This connects with the company's growth strategy and is a business growth metric, rather than a vanity metric that could apply to any organisation.

- The work is **timed** so that the measurement can take place and you can see how effective the objective has been within 12 months.

It's important to note that the example in Figure 4.2 shows *what* needs to be done to achieve this strategy, but not *how*. It does not provide a list of tactics, such as by using social media, gaining more likes, sending newsletters – these are tactics that are considered in <u>STEP 6</u> when we build the plan.

Having understood the different elements of SMART as well as how to construct a strong objective, it's your turn.

Annmarie's Advice

When you write a SMART objective, you do not need to explain every element as I have done here (that's granulating); you simply need to create an objective that is SMART, like the example in Figure 4.2

4.3 Refine your objective

In activity 4.2 you reviewed your first objective; look back again and check that it's SMART.

Write the objective here and use arrows to identify the SMART elements in the same way as the example in Figure 4.2:

Strengths and weaknesses in the SMART elements

You may or may not have covered all the SMART elements; let's explore these further and consider some examples.

Specific

The objective must be specific which means that there should be one clear purpose – not several. It should be focused on the company, not a generic or broad goal which could be applied to any organisation. An example of a weak objective that is generic is 'increase web visitors by 50 per cent over six months' – that sounds like an objective every company wants! How does this make a material difference to an organisation?

Weak objectives contain multiple items and are often very long; with many sentences, instead of one. The test is whether you can repeat the objective to a colleague.

Measurable

A form of measurement must be included so that you know when you've reached your goal. This is about quantifying the objective which can involve increasing numbers or growing percentages of items, such as those shown in Table 4.2.

Measurement example	Strategy	Impact on the company
Email subscriptions	Consideration and conversion	Building the database allows for the potential to increase sales
Conversion rate	Conversion	Gaining sales or data, such as email addresses
Ratings/Reviews	Enthusiasm	Enabling other customers to spread the word to lead to other conversions

Table 4.2 Examples of measures

These measures are meaningful because they have an impact on the company and are thus considered strong metrics.

In digital marketing, many companies use an analytics program, such as Google Analytics. This contains significant **metrics** about all aspects of the customer journey, including: visitor locations, sources of web traffic, top performing content, the number of visitors that made a purchase, the number that started a purchase but abandoned their cart, how the visitors found the website and their behaviour on site (pages visited, top exit pages) and much more.

> 4.4 Try the Google Analytics Demo account
>
> To learn how to use Google Analytics, you can access a fully working free demonstration account. It allows you to look at real data, explore the different metrics and try out Google Analytics.
>
> Search 'Google Analytics Demo account' for more details.

For much more on metrics and the NPS, see Digital Marketing: Strategic Planning & Integration by Annmarie Hanlon

To measure customer satisfaction, many companies use external measurement systems, such as the Net Promoter Score® (NPS) which gives a score out of 100 based on different factors.

Another example of a strong objective is from **ASOS**, which has targets to keep customers happy. As part of a retention strategy, the objective could be 'To improve customer satisfaction by 10 per cent by December'. This objective is SMART and describes what is needed to achieve the strategy but does not say how. The company already has a measurement system in place as it uses the NPS system and this would be further detailed when building the action plan.

Weak metrics are those that are unlikely to make a real difference to the company and may not have been discovered as a critical factor in the earlier research. For example, an objective 'to gain 100 more likes in two months' is unlikely to change the company. Just because people like the social media page, it doesn't mean they are customers!

It's important to reflect on whether the objective is based on earlier research and relevant to the company. Did the PESTLE or competitor analysis indicate that gaining more likes would make a difference?

Achievable

Achievable is sometimes referred to as attainable, or whether this is practical for the company. To be achievable, an objective must also be relevant. You would be unlikely to suggest that Zoom could deliver 10,000 kiosks to universities in six months. Zoom may not yet have the resources for this as it would involve a strategic move from software to hardware that wasn't identified in the earlier research as a factor. Objectives should apply to the company's abilities and be connected to the earlier research.

To make an objective relevant, return to **STEP 1** and **STEP 2** and check whether the objective is based on your earlier research. Also consider the personas and whether they should be included.

Realistic

A realistic objective is one that can be completed by the company. This is about whether it can be fulfilled in the time allowed. If you were asked to create a digital marketing plan in two hours, this may not be realistic! If you were given two weeks, it may be a challenge, but could be completed.

Weak objectives are those that are unlikely to be carried out as they are so far from reality. For example, if a company that typically has 150 sales a month wants to gain 1,000 more sales within one day, this may not be realistic!

Timed

A timeframe should be included so that the objective can be assessed at a later time. It's a little like an assignment – your first question is always: 'What's the hand-in date?' Companies are no different and need to know the timeframe to plan the work.

4.5 Find the weak or strong objectives

Consider the objectives in this table and identify whether they are weak or strong and explain why:

Example objective	Strong or weak?	Why is this?
1. To gain brand awareness		
2. To get more visitors to the website by September		
3. To increase web visitors by 10% in 12 months		
4. To organise 3 events by the end of December		
5. To provide information for customers		
6. To improve online conversion by 2% by the end of the year		
7. To write more blog articles in December		
8. To increase sales by 2000% in two months		

* The answers are at the end of this Step.

Examples of weak objectives

Here are some examples of weak objectives to help show what you should avoid doing:

Increase sales by 25 per cent

This is not a SMART objective. There is no timeframe which means that the objective never ends. It is not clear what is meant by sales – all the products the company sells, or just one product group? It lacks context, so whether it is realistic is not clear.

This would be better written as:

- To increase sales of online training by 25 per cent within eight months.

Work on search engine optimisation to deliver a better organic reach by appearing on page 1 of Google for the top ten key search words, resulting in a 10 per cent increase of website visitors during the period of July compared with the previous month, measured through Google Analytics

This is a poorly constructed set of multiple objectives and activities stuck together, and it is not SMART! This is known as a nested objective with multiple items, including how the objective will be achieved, stuck together.

For example, 'Work on search engine optimisation' seems to be the action and 'to deliver a better organic reach' seems to be the aim, so this lacks clarity.

The intended outcome of 'appearing on page 1 of Google for the top ten key search words' is not realistic and shows a lack of understanding of how Google works – being at the top of Google is often time-limited and depends on many factors (competitors, budget available, search for those keywords).

The additional outcome '10 per cent increase of website visitors' demonstrates that this is a 'nested' or 'multiple' objective – one added to another, inside another, which means that the objective lacks clarity and is not specific as it contains multiple outcomes.

The action takes place over one month which seems unrealistic for such a large ambition. Although the measurement tool has been included (Google Analytics), this is not needed and would be a level of detail considered at the planning stage.

This would be better written as two objectives:

- To increase website visitors by 10 per cent within six months

- To improve the ranking of our top ten key search words by 25 per cent within six months

To gain 100 more likes from Facebook and Instagram

This is not an objective, but a digital marketing activity. Plus, it is not clear if this means 100 new Facebook likes *and* 100 new Instagram likes, or 50 from Facebook and 50 from Instagram?

There is another question which is whether this has a major impact on the growth of the company. It is unlikely that this would make a significant difference. Most social media platforms allow companies to 'buy likes' in the advertising centre, by promoting their page to a relevant potential audience – allow $1 per like, but liking a page doesn't mean that business will grow. The super car Lamborghini has over 12 million likes on Facebook but sells fewer than 10,000 cars a year. Likes do not always represent customers!

As these examples show, they lack clarity and are not SMART. Having considered the different aspects of strong objectives and understood the elements in weaker objectives, it's over to you! Start with three objectives and remember to go back to the earlier steps to check your notes.

4.6 Create three SMART objectives for your company

Use the table as a structure to build your objectives.

Objectives	Rationale	Policy	Digital marketing strategy

Summary

This step looked at constructing SMART objectives based on earlier steps. Stronger objectives use the strategy so that they are relevant and appropriate for the company. If the objectives are weak, it may be that you need to review the strategy to ensure that it is clear.

You have now:

1. Assessed the organisation's background and drawn conclusions
2. Analysed the audience to create personas
3. Created your digital marketing strategy
4. Constructed relevant objectives

The next step is explaining how this will be funded, who will do the work and when.

Notes:

_____

_____

_____

_____

_____

_____

_____

_____

_____

_____

_____

_____

_____

_____

_____

_____

_____

_____

Answers to Activity 4.5

	Example objective	Strong or weak?	Why is this?
1.	To gain brand awareness	Weak	It is not specific, not measurable and not timed
2.	To get more visitors to the website by September	Weak	Although it's timed, it's not measurable, so more visitors could include just one person!
3.	To increase web visitors by 10% in 12 months	Strong	This is a SMART objective
4.	To organise three events by the end of December	Weak	This includes measurement and timing but it is a tactic rather than an objective
5.	To provide information for customers	Weak	This is vague – what information, where and when and why? Is this a tactic or an objective? It is not clear
6.	To improve online conversion by 2% by the end of the year	Strong	This is a SMART objective
7.	To write more blog articles in December	Weak	This is an activity, not an objective. We don't know why these blog articles are needed and how they contribute to the strategy
8.	To increase sales by 2000% in two months	Weak	This is specific, measurable and timed but it may not be realistic for the company or may be impossible to achieve in two months – it took TikTok five years to grow by 900%

STEP 5

JUSTIFY THE
RESOURCES

At this time, your digital marketing plan is taking shape. You understand and have researched the context and company background, you've analysed the audience, created a strategy and developed the objectives. That is all fantastic, but what resources are needed to make it happen? How does this work?

Justifying resources means explaining why specific items are needed. Do you remember asking family members for extra money for an item? Did you create a story as to why the money was needed and why it was so important? It's the same in business. You should demonstrate what is needed and clearly explain why. You may need to show arguments for and against other options if you are asked to evaluate a situation.

The 9Ms

It is helpful to use a framework when creating the initial list of resources. This ensures that you don't miss something that you need later.

In the textbook *Digital Marketing: Strategic Planning & Integration*, I suggested a resources model, the 9Ms, shown in Figure 5.1, that is based on an earlier manufacturing model for resources – the 3Ms. The reason I extended the resources from the 3Ms – men, money and minutes (or time, people and budgets) – is that in a digital environment more resources are needed, such as materials for content (images, words, videos) or machines (webcams, apps or subscriptions for online services), and all the actions need to be clearly explained.

Let's explore each of these resource factors.

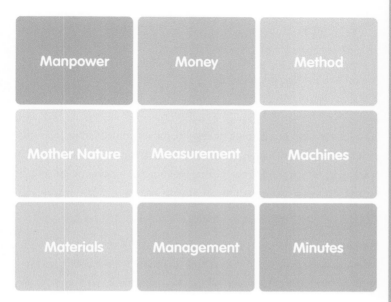

Figure 5.1 The 9Ms

Manpower – People or roles

The people needed in a digital environment may be more than marketing managers and agencies. It's important to be specific about who will do the work so that any gaps in people planning can be identified as early as possible. Other roles that may be relevant include copywriters, graphic designers, video editors and social media managers.

Consider all the roles that are needed to achieve your objective. In the Zoom objective 'To gain referrals from 30 per cent of Jones Family customers within 12 months', two roles that may be needed are:

- Customer service executives – to contact the customers
- Copywriters – to create emails to be sent to the customers

If the work will be conducted in-house, think about whether any of the team need further training and add this to the budget.

Annmarie's Advice

A weak digital marketing plan fails to add costs for social media. Social media posts and content are never free – people are needed to plan, create and post the content!

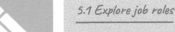

There are many new roles emerging; for example, TikTok job roles include 'Customer Success Manager Trust & Safety', 'Entertainment Marketing Intern' and 'Emergency Response' – none of these are typical job roles, but reflect the changing nature of digital marketing.

Money – Budget and finances

Marketing budgets can be connected to (a) the amount needed to meet the objectives, (b) the available finances, (c) last year's budget, or (d) percentage of turnover, which is usually between 5 and 20 per cent depending on the company type.

The budget should be relevant to the company, so suggesting a budget of £1 million for a company with a turnover of £2 million is not realistic. Just because the total sales income (turnover) is £2 million, does not mean the company can spend this income. The gross profit may be 50 per cent – that's £1 million – but then there are other expenses, such as salaries, general administration costs, expenditure on research and development, as well as ensuring there is (contingency) money in the bank in case of unforeseen or international disasters.

A technology organisation with annual sales of £1 billion might spend £10 million a year with a well-known advertising agency, but this would only be part of its whole marketing budget, which is likely to be £200 million – or 20 per cent of revenue. The company may also use multiple advertising agencies in different locations. So, if you recommend a campaign that costs £10,000, this may be too low, unless it is a pilot campaign to test a concept.

Trying to suggest a budget for a company is challenging if you are not working there, so you may need to estimate, based on the evidence and research. This also requires some understanding of the costs of digital marketing materials.

> ### 5.2 Explore company budgets
>
> Companies with investors have to provide annual reports – these contain more details about their revenue and expenditure. Search online for 'company name + investors', download their latest annual report and you'll be able to see their sales income, expenditure and learn more about their budgets.

For example, looking online at its annual report, I discovered that in 2020 Zoom's net income was over $25 million. This means that a total marketing budget, based on 5 per cent of income, would be $1.25 million. So, if I am recommending a budget of $150,000 to $200,000 a year for my digital marketing plan, this is 1 to 16 per cent of the total marketing budget and so it's not unrealistic as the main budget may have been allocated for other plans.

Annmarie's Advice

When you're preparing a budget, stick to one currency

Method – Approach to the work

This concerns the approach to carry out the work, which can be in-house, or outsourced to an agency, or to other third parties.

Key factors to consider:

- In-house does not mean it is free! As a minimum, you need to pay salaries; although these are not usually included in a marketing budget, they should be acknowledged.

- If you are using an agency, be specific about what type of agency and which roles are involved. Weak plans often state

'outsourced to an agency', but they don't explain what type of agency and who will deliver the work. There are ad agencies, PR agencies, design agencies, brand agencies, digital agencies, SEO agencies, influencer agencies, full-service agencies and others we haven't yet considered!

5.3 The cost of outsourcing

When outsourcing, you are paying for the time of experts with great contacts, so if you're engaging a PR or content management agency in the UK, it's likely that the starting budget will be £25,000, but £100,000 for a major brand is not unusual.

What it costs is a frequently asked question and to learn more visit quora.com and search for questions such as:

- How much does it cost to hire an ad agency?
- How do creative agencies charge?

Mother Nature – External unforeseen factors

Mother Nature influences so many business decisions, such as types of organisation, customer groups, products offered and business location. For example, **Helly Hansen**, the Norwegian performance clothing brand, was started by a sea captain who needed better clothing to face Mother Nature. The product was a direct result of the local environment.

During the COVID-19 pandemic, major **French perfume houses** such as Christian Dior and Louis Vuitton adapted to Mother Nature and started manufacturing hand sanitiser.

5.4 The impact of Mother Nature

In groups, discuss examples of organisations starting – or closing – as a result of Mother Nature.

Depending on the business type and location, you may need to address local environmental circumstances in your digital marketing plan. For example, if your website offers:

- Restaurant bookings only – add an option for takeaway services in case the economy shrinks

- Technology that needs superfast internet – add a low bandwidth option for when it slows down

Measurement – Assessing the results

When allocating resources, it's essential to assess the results to see how well they worked. The approach to measurement depends on the objectives.

Let's return to the Zoom case and look at one of the earlier objectives and assess how the results can be measured.

Objectives	Metric	Calculating the measurement	Tools
To convert 20% of Alex and Fraser customers from freemium to paid-for subscriptions within 12 months	An additional 20%	Take a benchmark of the current customers in this group, calculate 20% to determine the increase	Customer database, Google Analytics

Table 5.1 Measurement of Zoom's objectives

The customer database is often referred to as the CRM – the customer relationship management system. Often, it's a list of customers, their contact details and sometimes their purchase history. More sophisticated CRM systems can identify when purchases are made (e.g. around pay day) and the average spend per customer. CRM systems can be useful tools to benchmark data.

If we assume that Zoom has 100 million people using the system and 10 per cent of these are premium customers, that's 10 million. This means that 20 per cent of this group is an additional 2 million paid-for customers (the calculation is 10,000,000 x 0.2 = 2,000,000).

That's a lot of new customers to track, so we need an intelligent – and easier – way of doing this.

We can use a dedicated landing page that contains tracking code that we can view in Google Analytics. This will allow us to see (a) how many people visited the page and (b) how many people clicked through to become premium customers. Each month we can run a report to measure the results, using Google Analytics as our measurement tool.

Using Google Analytics is one tool available and this will also assess the number of web visitors or the most popular web pages. Other measurement tools we may consider include:

- Pay-per-click results – how many people clicked on the advert, what the click-through rate was
- Content performance – how many people liked, shared or commented on the content we've added

The tools depend on the objective that you've created, so it's up to you to ensure that it's relevant.

5.5 Finding your measurement tools

Look back at the SMART objective created in Activity 4.3. Note the unit of measurement (what you are measuring) and the tools needed to measure this.

Digital marketing metrics and analytics is a large subject and while this planner shows you how to include measurement in your digital marketing plan, you may need to refer to *Digital Marketing: Strategic Planning & Integration* by Annmarie Hanlon for more on this subject.

Don't forget, although there are many forms of measurement, the one you choose must be based on the objectives!

Machines – Tools or equipment

If your objective is recommending in-house development of a new website, does the team delivering this have the right equipment? Sometimes referred to as **tools**, the machines are the instruments, programs or facilities needed to deliver the objectives.

Often, the machines needed are already available within the organisation, although during the pandemic many organisations needed to purchase equipment including webcams and green screens for staff working from home who needed them for online meetings.

Review whether new desktops or screens may be needed, or if they might need photographic or recording kit. They may need an investment in software or online apps and these items are also part of the machinery required to carry out the tasks.

For example, **Cisco Systems** is an American technology company that manufactures and sells computer hardware and software. As a B2B company, it uses Mailchimp email software to stay in touch with its customers and keep them up to date. If, like Cisco Systems, you're sending over 2,000 emails a month, you'll need an email campaign programme to manage the sending and to make unsubscribing easier.

5.6 Explore the costs of email software systems

Email software systems charge based on volume of usage, with fees ranging from £25 to £1,000 per month, however they can be free for less usage.

Search for 'email campaign programmes' and compare the different platforms and their charges. Make notes here and in the Scribble Space at the back of the book!

Make notes here:

Read the chapter 'Content Marketing' in Digital Marketing: Strategic Planning & Integration by Annmarie Hanlon

Materials – Digital content

This is a key factor in digital marketing and often overlooked as a resource. Websites, email, online ads, social media posts and blog articles all require words, images and video – this is digital content.

Images for use in social media and on websites can be licensed via online image websites and some companies may have an in-house photographer, or engage a photographer when needed.

Content production is recognised as a digital job role and companies like ASOS employ content specialists who are 'responsible for the creation, delivery and optimisation of all onsite content pages'.

Digital content takes time and effort to create which is why companies encourage customers to create content – user-generated content, as well as employing influencers to produce more materials. This co-creation alleviates the burden of producing all new materials but introduces additional work – managing the influencers. This has created roles such as 'Influencer marketing executives' who recruit, build relationships with and report on influencer performance.

Unless the company has an in-house team with the time available for additional work, some of the digital content may need to be outsourced or bought from third parties such as advertising and design agencies. This role often involves creating the materials, from organising photo shoots to preparing imagery and video, all of which needs to be included in the budget.

5.7 The cost of materials

To better understand the costs in producing these materials, search for:

- 'online images' to see the different subscription options in image websites
- 'content creators' for an indication of blog writing fees
- 'product photography costs' for an estimate of the fees involved in creating lifestyle imagery

Management – Senior supporters

It can be challenging to gain budget sign-off unless there is a senior sponsor or supporter who can help.

The role of this person is to support and recommend your proposals – and your digital marketing plan, to the senior management team. If you are part of the senior management team, identify an ally who can also support you. This always helps when recommending new actions as well as financial requirements.

It's a good idea to share your plan with your management supporter before any formal meeting, so they have a chance to provide feedback and any suggestions.

5.8 Identify your management supporter

If you're working at a company and creating this plan for them, identify the person that's most likely to be the management supporter. This could be your line manager or the person who hired you (if that was someone different) or perhaps a senior colleague.

Minutes – Timescales

Think back to your last assignment. Did you need more time? Would an extra day have helped? This is why it's essential to think through the real amount of time needed to deliver an objective.

When you are working at a company, there is often an additional factor – securing approval. So, although you have a campaign ready to launch (the agency took two weeks to create it, you responded with some changes, these were made and after four weeks it is ready to go), you will most likely need other people to 'sign off' and confirm

Annmarie's Advice

Make sure you allow sufficient time to achieve the objectives in your digital marketing plan

the campaign is relevant for their audience and their strategy. This all takes time. People are in meetings, then more meetings and it may take a week (or two) just to gain clearance and permission to go ahead!

Consider the variables and the number of people involved in your recommended objectives, then factor in the timescales when creating your digital marketing plan.

5.9 Estimate the time needed

When third parties are involved, it always takes longer to finish a project. As an example, search online for: 'How long does it take to build a website?'.

Identifying the required resources

When you have identified and justified the required resources, this should relate back to the earlier objectives as they are the driving force behind the plan. This helps to ensure that nothing is missing.

Figure 5.2 shows the resources needed for two of my Zoom objectives that were explained in STEP 4. They are numbered so it's easier to see which resources are needed for which objectives. This means that it's easier to look back at the earlier work to see the connections.

The method will involve in-house teams as well as agencies and freelancers, which need to be considered in the budget. Mother Nature is not included as it is not relevant for these objectives. I have mentioned machines as, although these are not required, it's possible a colleague may think I've forgotten this element.

5.10 Identify the required resources for two of your company's objectives

Don't forget, you'll need to outline the required resources for all of your objectives in your full digital marketing plan!

Objective 1

Objective 2

Objective 1. Gain referrals from customers

- People: Roles to set up and manage the referral programme and process; a digital marketing manager, an assistant and possibly agency staff

- Budget: An agency to create the referral programme and launch – allow $35,000

  - Ongoing email campaigns – allow $500 per month
  - Website landing page – allow $2,000 to design and build

- Machines: None identified

- Materials: Imagery needed for all content – allow $5,000 and this can be used in other campaigns

(Continued)

Objective 2. Convert from freemium to paid

- People: Existing staff can manage this through the CRM and email platforms, but some training will be needed – allow $2,000

- Budget: Salesforce CRM software to manage data – $300 per user, per month; assume 30 users, $9,000 per month or $108,000 per year

  - Social media ads targeted at Alex and Fraser personas – allow $10,000

- Machines: None identified

- Materials: Salesforce CRM already identified

Figure 5.2 Examples of resources for Zoom objectives

The budget

When you've created the lists of items, for each objective, the costs can be identified and added into a separate budget, as shown in Table 5.2. This notes all the costs and, where relevant, the monthly charges are included, along with a final total.

Annmarie's Advice

It's important to include a summary of the final budget in a digital marketing plan as this saves the person reading your work the time to calculate it

Item	Per month	Total $
Agency to create referral programme and launch		35,000
Training for existing staff		2,000
Ongoing email campaigns	500	6,000
Website landing page		2,000

Salesforce CRM software	9,000	108,000
Social media ads		10,000
Imagery		5,000
TOTAL		**168,000**

Table 5.2 Zoom budget for objectives 1 and 2

Notes:

_____

_____

_____

_____

_____

_____

_____

_____

_____

_____

_____

_____

_____

_____

_____

_____

_____

_____

_____

5.11 Outline the budget

Use this table to note the main costs involved to achieve your recommended objectives:

Item	Per month	Total
GRAND TOTAL		

Summary

STEP 5 involved justifying the resources. To do this, several additional steps were taken:

Annmarie's Advice

Ensure that the recommended resources link directly back to the objectives and are therefore valid!

- Identifying the different resources to be considered using the 9M model as a framework

- Applying the 9Ms to the earlier objectives, which provided an indication as to which elements were and were not needed

Finally, having identified all the elements, a budget was created. The next step is about getting other people involved and building the plan.

Notes:

STEP 6

BUILD THE
ACTION PLAN

This step is constructing the action plan which is more than creating a document – it also consists in getting other people, the stakeholders, involved, so that the plan has a greater chance of success. Let's explore who the stakeholders may be before building the plan.

Stakeholder mapping

We can define **stakeholders** as those individuals, organisations or business units with a stake or an interest in the activity.

For example, within your university the stakeholders include the students, academic and support staff, alumni, suppliers, local community, government bodies and others, depending on the university's location.

To make it easier to identify who is a stakeholder, we can create a stakeholder map (based on an idea from researchers Freeman and McVea in 2005), like the example shown in Figure 6.1.

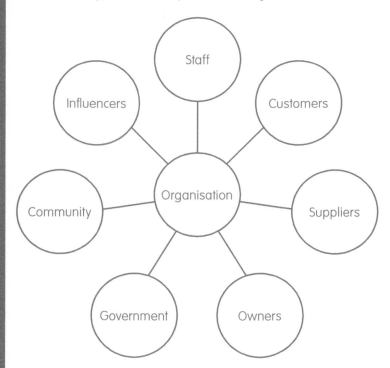

Figure 6.1   Stakeholder map example

Figure 6.1 is a simplistic map, and a good place to start as it highlights the main groups involved. There may be many changes or extensions to the stakeholder map, depending on the organisation's context, current plans and environment.

Mendelow (1981) mentioned that the stakeholders make contributions to the organisation in exchange for something. For example:

- Staff work for the firm and are paid a salary

- Investors provide funding in exchange for a return at a later date

- Suppliers provide goods in return for payment

Competitors are sometimes included in a stakeholder map as they have a stake in the organisation, although Mendelow felt that competitors do not make a contribution but instead seek to gain from stakeholders. For example, competitors may wish to entice staff to work for them and bring commercial knowledge, or encourage suppliers to give them the enhanced terms, or attract influencers to promote their products.

We addressed competitors as a separate group in STEP 1, so they are not included in Figure 6.1.

Notes:

_____

_____

_____

_____

_____

_____

_____

_____

_____

_____

6.1 Create a stakeholder map

Think about your case organisation and create a basic stakeholder map using the blank template. Add extra circles if needed and don't forget to check back to STEP 5 and look at the people resources required – they should be included here!

Annmarie's Advice

If your plan involves different departments, make sure they're added to your stakeholder map so you can consider how to engage these stakeholders

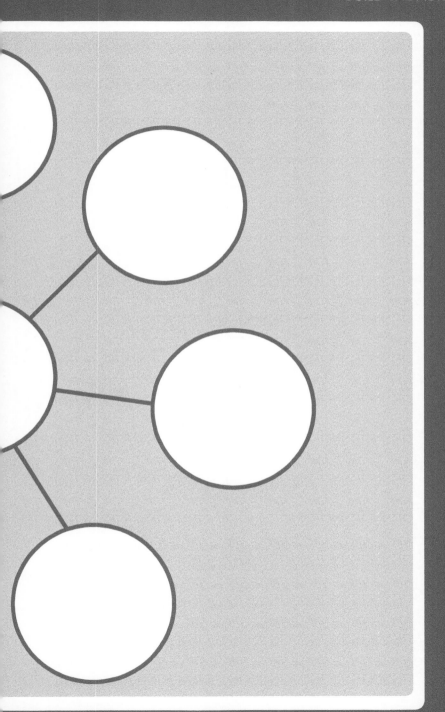

Using Zoom as an example, Figure 6.2 shows another example of a stakeholder map. Based on my knowledge of Zoom, this includes investors too – they're the people funding the growth of the business, so they have a keen interest in its activities.

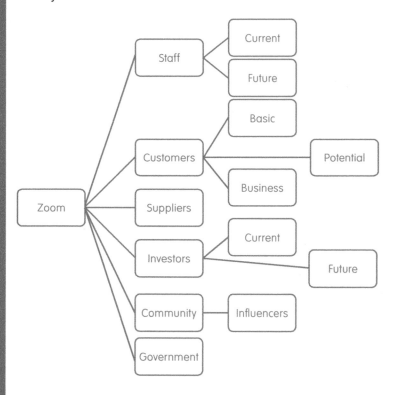

Figure 6.2 Zoom stakeholder map

Figure 6.2 starts to explore the different staff involved in the process by adding in two groups: current and future.

In your stakeholder map, you may granulate the different groups, adding further detail. For example, you could extend the staff element to include the business units involved with your action plan – namely the management team, marketing team and others who may have an impact on the project. Or you could add others in their environment, such as governing bodies who regulate communication activities in different locations.

The power/interest matrix

Having created the stakeholder map, what do you do with it? Back in 1981, Professor Aubrey L. Mendelow created a stakeholder model that was based on the amount of power or interest that the stakeholder had in the organisation. This is often called the 'Mendelow Matrix' (Mendelow, 1981) and an example of this is shown in Figure 6.3.

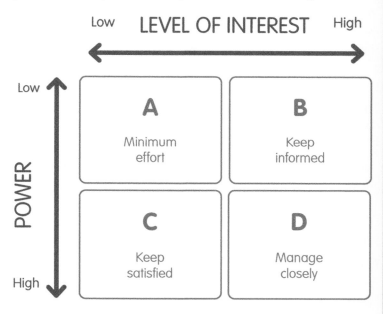

Figure 6.3   The power/interest matrix

Source: Adapted from Mendelow (1981)

This is a classic 2 x 2 matrix that includes two reference points – power and interest. These are classified as being from high to low, resulting in four groups which I'll explain and connect back to the Zoom example.

A - Power low, level of interest low

Mendelow recommended that minimum effort was needed to keep this group updated, so being on an email list and gaining updates every month may be acceptable.

For Zoom, this group may include suppliers providing office services, such as water coolers. Zoom may not be their biggest customer and they are more concerned with larger offices, so their interest is low and their authority or power over Zoom is also low. There is no need to include them in the process at this time.

B - Power low, level of interest high

These stakeholders may not have power, but they are interested, so it's wise to keep them informed and included in activities which may affect them.

For example, these may be basic Zoom customers who don't pay for the service and want to watch and see if the free service changes. Regular updates, such as newsletters, may be helpful.

C - Power high, level of interest low

Those with high levels of power need to be kept in the loop.

With Zoom, this could include early investors who provided funds but are now working with much larger organisations. They want to know their money is safe; they don't want daily updates but they will need full financial information at quarterly intervals.

D - Power high, level of interest high

This is the most powerful group and they have been described as those who should be managed closely or kept informed of the details on a regular basis.

Thinking about the Zoom example, this could include members of the senior management team who are committed to the organisation but also possess key knowledge or skills, which is why they have high levels of power. This group needs monthly updates and will have a keen interest in this digital marketing plan.

6.2 Develop a power/interest matrix

Using your stakeholder map as a starting point, create a power/interest matrix for your case organisation.
You can use the blank template or create your own version.

LEVEL OF INTEREST

Low — High

POWER

Low — High

Gantt charts

Having identified who needs to be kept updated and involved, the next stage involves producing the action plan for those involved to follow.

One approach is to use a **Gantt chart**, which is a popular project management tool. It is named after Henry Gantt who created the concept over 100 years ago (Gantt, 1919) for use in manufacturing production processes. Typically, these included activities and timescales (what and when). They are commonly used and have been updated to include more detail, such as people and budget (who and how much).

A Gantt chart could be described as a timed list of all granulated activities and all the tactics, including the roles for the work.

Gantt charts cannot be created until you have all the pieces of the jigsaw together along with clear objectives which you developed in STEP 4. To create a Gantt chart, start with one objective and extract every action needed to make this happen.

Returning to Zoom, Table 6.1 shows an example of a Gantt chart, using the earlier objectives created in STEP 4

The budget details are excluded as they have already been noted in a separate budget table (see Table 5.2). Activities to review and report on the results have also been included in this chart. These are based on the timing in the objectives, and there are some earlier reviews in place in case the plans need to be adapted.

By adding in the objectives, you are linking this back to earlier work and making it easier for colleagues to understand why each action is needed.

Gantt charts have existed for over 100 years which may be one of the reasons they are so well known and so well used. They show, at a glance, the amount of work needed to achieve the objectives. Plus, they work well online and can also be printed out to pin on a wall.

The content in the Gantt chart may include promotional or communication activities. Consider elements of the Digital Marketing toolbox in the main textbook to help with this.

6.3 Create a Gantt chart for two of your objectives

Create a Gantt chart by using spreadsheet software, such as Google Sheets, Microsoft Excel or Apple Numbers:

Column A – Add the objectives

Column B – Add the details

Column C – Add who will do the work

Column D–I – Add in six months of the timescale

This may look like the example from Excel and you can refine and improve the presentation.

A	B	C	D	E	F	G	H	I
				Timescale in months				
Objective	Details	People	1	2	3	4	5	6

Figure 6.4 Example of the top of a Gantt chart

Objective	Detail	Who (role)
1.	Prepare brief	Digital marketing manager
	Create programme	Agency account manager to lead
	Review programme	Digital marketing manager
	Confirm and approve	Marketing director
	Design website landing page	Web team (CX, graphics roles)
	Build website landing page	Web developer
	Launch and promote campaign	Digital marketing manager
2.	Provide training for salesforce	Digital marketing assistant
	Create campaign overview and brief	Digital marketing manager
	Plan social media ads	Social media executive
	Plan email copy and sequences	Email manager
	Create social media ads	Content creator
	Create email copy	Digital marketing executive
	Confirm and approve social media ads and emails	Digital marketing manager
1 & 2	Review results	Digital marketing manager
	Report results to the management team	Digital marketing manager
	Evaluate the results	Digital marketing manager

Table 6.1 Zoom action plan for objectives 1 and 2

					Month						
1	2	3	4	5	6	7	8	9	10	11	12

The program evaluation and review technique (PERT)

Gantt charts have been criticised for being too simple and sometimes considered as basic bar charts. Consequently, other techniques have emerged, such as the program evaluation and review technique (PERT) which was created by the United States Navy when building a submarine! Clearly, that project needed many more activities and the PERT included cumulative expenses to show the total project cost (Management Systems Corporation, 1961). Figure 6.5 shows a simple example of PERT that was created using PowerPoint flowchart shapes.

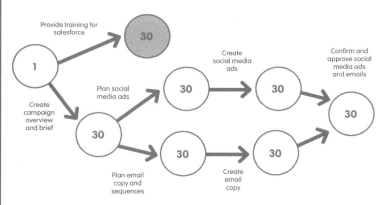

Figure 6.5 Simple example of PERT

Figure 6.5 uses Zoom Objective 2 – convert from freemium to paid. In Objective 2 there are initially seven activities. The work starts on day 1 and one month is considered as 30 days.

One disadvantage of this example is that, unless I make it more complicated, it excludes *who* is doing the work. Another downside is that detailed costings are needed for it to be successful.

An advantage is that it highlights that one activity, 'Provide training for salesforce', is not picked up later. So, why is it needed? Perhaps it would be better to refine the Gantt chart at this stage to add 'Use salesforce to monitor results'. The PERT also shows more clearly the dependencies between one action and another.

The advantage of a more complex version of PERT is that it recognises that timescales can change and often includes three levels of timings that are: (a) planned or scheduled, (b) worst-case or pessimistic, and (c) best-case or optimistic timescales, enabling project managers to adjust other factors where needed.

However, both Gantt and PERT have contributed to many project management tools that are available online.

6.4 Search online for free project management tools

To see what's available, search online for 'Gantt chart maker free' or 'free online PERT chart maker'.

You may discover other project management tools or templates to use online or to download.

Compare with colleagues to discover what's easiest to use, looks professional and can be read by your teachers or examiners.

Make further notes in the Scribble Space at the back of the book!

I'm recommending a spreadsheet but there are other tools also available online. For example, Trello.com allows you to create and share a plan with others. It's based on a visual system where you create cards, assign roles and move the cards as the work is completed, but it doesn't work for printed documents, so may be less helpful for an assignment you have to submit.

Summary

STEP 6 involved building the action plan. This started with stakeholder mapping to identify who was involved with the digital marketing plan. From this, the power/interest matrix was introduced to indicate where most effort was needed in stakeholder communications.

Having identified and classified the stakeholders, Gantt charts were discussed as a method of building the action plan, as well as the program evaluation and review technique (PERT). Examples of a Gantt chart and a PERT diagram were included.

Having created most of the digital marketing plan, the next steps act as a checking system to ensure we assess whether the plan has worked.

Notes:

_____

_____

_____

_____

_____

_____

_____

_____

_____

_____

_____

_____

_____

_____

_____

_____

_____

STEP 7

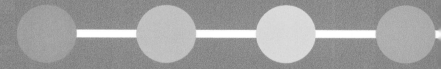

EVALUATE
THE PLAN

Once you have completed **STEP 6** and created your action plan, we've nearly reached the end of the journey, but how do we know if the plan is a success or not?

To **evaluate** means to judge, assess, appraise or measure. This is a critical aspect of marketing and planning, whether that's online or offline. Being able to decode metrics is becoming an essential part of many marketing jobs.

Why do we need evaluation?

Evaluating the plan is closing the loop, measuring results and understanding what worked well – and what worked less well. The aim of this is to inform future plans to ensure they are constantly improved.

However, it's easier to evaluate when you have a benchmark or measure at the start. This is why we added measurable factors into the objectives in **STEP 4**.

Let's first unravel the terminology. Table 7.1 shows the differences between metrics, analytics and insights.

Term	What this means	For example
Metrics	A unit of measurement	Percentage, numbers of, volume of web visitors
Analytics	Analysing the data	Interpreting why visitor numbers to the website drop on Mondays
Insights	Explaining why	Reviewing the environment to see if external factors impact web visitor behaviour

Table 7.1 Metrics, analytics and insights

Metrics

We'll explore metrics first and consider the different types available.

However, what's essential is that for the metrics to work, you need a *benchmark* or point of reference. You need to assess where you are before deciding where to go!

For example, if **Just Eat Takeaway.com** announced that it would increase its app downloads by 10 per cent, you have to know how many downloads there were at the start to understand what 10 per cent looks like.

Let's suggest that there have been 25 million downloads; this is our benchmark. So this means that 10 per cent growth represents an extra 2.5 million.

If Just Eat Takeaway.com gains an additional 2 million downloads in the agreed timescale, although it has grown by 8 per cent, the firm hasn't achieved its objective, so the metrics suggest that the plan was not totally successful for some reason.

On the other hand, if the company had a further 3 million downloads in the planned timetable, this is more than expected as it represents 12 per cent growth. Therefore, the objective has been accomplished and we can say the plan was successful based on this metric.

Annmarie's Advice

Make sure that you've suggested benchmarks at the start, as this allows you to evaluate these metrics later in the plan

7.1 Suggest the benchmarks

Return to STEP 4 *to see the objectives that you recommended. What were these metrics based on? Did you have benchmarks?*

Make notes here:

Objectives as metrics

If you have created SMART objectives in Step 4, these are a useful way of evaluating a plan because these measurements can be assessed.

But if your objectives aren't SMART and are missing the 'M' in measurable, you'll need to review them and ensure this is included.

For example, using the Zoom objectives in Table 4.1, did we:

- gain referrals from 30 per cent of Jones Family customers within 12 months?

- convert 20 per cent of Alex and Fraser customers from freemium to paid-for subscriptions within 12 months?

Hard and soft measures

Objectives are a helpful way to evaluate a plan, but there are more ways to assess whether an action was successful or not. We can divide these into hard and soft measures.

Hard measures

These are quantifiable and based on specific numbers. When using hard measures, no other metric is needed to assess the results.

An example of a hard measure is a percentage or an increase in numbers, such as to increase customers by 10 per cent, similar to the Just Eat Takeaway.com example above. It is straightforward to assess and evaluate whether the objective has been achieved.

Soft measures

These are often qualitative and so they are open to interpretation. They may involve changes in behaviour, increases in brand awareness or feelings about an organisation.

How customers feel about a brand can be a soft measure and difficult to gauge. This is why many companies use polls or surveys to gather opinions, so they can gather some data to build a case that can be evaluated at a later stage. To do this, we need some additional techniques and tools which are outlined in Table 7.2.

Techniques	Tools
Quantitative	Online surveys, online polls
Qualitative	Online interviews

Table 7.2 Main evaluation techniques and tools

Another technique is to mix the quantitative and the qualitative to enrich the data, but this requires more time than using one alone. Let's investigate these tools.

Online surveys

Online surveys can be used to explore the opinions of existing customers, to gather information from potential customers and to test all aspects of the extended marketing mix.

Online surveys can be free or low cost and can be quick to run. There are a range of tools available and many of these, in their paid-for versions, provide options for data export so that the data can be extracted as a spreadsheet for further analysis. Online surveys can be distributed via website, email, social media and on blogs.

There are also disadvantages with online surveys as within the free tools there may be limits on the number of questions or participants.

Another disadvantage is 'survey fatigue' where customers are less keen on responding to 'yet another survey'. To counter this you might think of ways to reduce this; for example:

- Limit the number of surveys issued, with no more than one or two a year.

- Introduce an incentive. Incentives should be explained at the start and may include 10 per cent off, or a free gift with your next order. Zoom could offer 'a free upgrade for one month'.

- Partner with another company and issue a combined survey.

7.2 Search for survey tools

Search online for 'survey tools' to see more about the pricing and the different options available.

Make notes here about what you discovered:

You can find more space for notes in the Scribble Space at the back of the book!

Online polls

These are similar to online surveys but often shorter and limited to two, three or four questions. As with online surveys, the advantages are that online polls are quick to run and can be embedded in an email or a website pop-up.

The downside is that polls are quite basic. A very simple yes or no response limits how and where it can be used, as well as the depth of the data.

Online interviews

Online interviews can take place in varied formats, for example using Zoom, WhatsApp or WeChat.

Disadvantages with online interviews include the time it takes to organise the meetings and ensuring the participants turn up at the agreed time! There may be potential issues with technology for participants to consider and you need trained interviewers to run the sessions.

You also need to consider the time it will take to analyse the responses, regardless of whether you've selected surveys, polls or interviews.

Let's return to my Zoom example and explore how we can evaluate whether the plan worked.

We start by considering the objectives that were developed in STEP 4. Considering the evaluation before finalising the plan is valuable as it shows whether all the objectives are strong, or whether some need to be reviewed and adjusted as they might not work.

Objective 1	To gain referrals from 30% of Jones Family customers within 12 months
Metric	Referrals from 30% of a persona group
Method of evaluation	Quantifiable results that can be measured
Tools (materials or machinery)	Website form
Mechanism	• Assign a code to existing customers to share • Count the number of codes used via a web sign-up form in the 'back-end' of the website or CRM system • Check the company has a CRM system that can incorporate codes and run reports

This is a strong objective that can be evaluated and therefore works.

Objective 2	To convert 20% of Alex and Fraser customers from freemium to paid-for subscriptions within 12 months
Metric	20% of a persona group
Method of evaluation	Quantifiable results that can be measured
Tools (materials or machinery)	Website form
Mechanism	Benchmark the number of freemium customers in this persona group and tag at the start of the campaign Run a report using the tag at the end of the campaign that includes 'products used' to assess the total number Check that the website can run reports to assess these details If not, a 'report module' may need to be added to the website

This is also a strong objective that can be evaluated and works.

Objective 3a	To launch Zoom in India within four months
Metric	Not clear
Method of evaluation	Not clear
Tools (materials or machinery)	Difficult to say as the objective is not clear
Mechanism	

This objective is impossible to evaluate! We need to define 'launch' and what this means.

To launch could mean (a) holding a party or (b) gaining one new customer – none of this would cover the costs of recruiting a team in India or pay for the management team to be present at the event.

We need to review this objective and be more specific.

This can be rephrased as 'To win 5,000 customers in India within four months'; let's see if this can be evaluated:

Objective 3b	To win 5,000 customers in India within four months
Metric	5,000 new customers in India
Method of evaluation	Quantifiable results that can be measured
Tools (materials or machinery)	Website form Check whether the CRM system includes countries as well as customer names and email details
Mechanism	Benchmark the number of customers in India and tag at the start of the campaign Ensure country tags are added to customers in the CRM system so the number in India at the start and finish of the campaign can be measured

This is now a strong objective that can be evaluated and works.

Now it's your turn. It's time to say how you will evaluate your plan!

Notes:

7.3 Review two of your objectives to demonstrate evaluation

Show how you will evaluate your plan using these tables.

OBJECTIVE 1

Metric
Method of evaluation
Tools
Mechanism

OBJECTIVE 2

Metric
Method of evaluation
Tools
Mechanism

Analytics

Once we have the metrics, we need to examine the information. Analytics is about analysing the data and this is most often viewed within tools such as:

- Google Analytics – this provides access to web data showing the audience, their behaviour on the website, and the source (acquisition) of the web visitors

- Social media analytics – often called insights (but they are not) this provides details on metrics such as the page likes, how far the posts have reached and which content has been more successful

- App data – this provides data on the number of downloads, the app usage, reviews added to app stores and more

These analytics packages summarise data in general and don't provide information about individuals as this would contravene ethical standards.

Notes:

_____

_____

_____

_____

_____

_____

_____

_____

_____

_____

_____

_____

7.4 Check your analytics

If you have a social media account, such as Twitter or Instagram, look at your analytics.

NB: You need to have 100+ followers on Instagram to gain analytics and they're available on the mobile app only. Twitter keeps analytics in the 'more' area and is only available in the desktop version.

Make notes here:

- What do your analytics tell you?
- What else would you like to know, but this isn't provided?
- What differences exist between the different analytics systems?

You can find more space for notes in the Scribble Space at the back of the book!

Returning to Zoom and its web analytics, staff will be able to see the _numbers_ of people who visited the website, not _who_ they are. Zoom will also be able to discover the main keywords used to find its website or the most successful blog articles its staff have created.

However, this data does not explain why – that's where insights are important.

Insights

Insights take the data that's been analysed or categorised and start to provide a story to give insight into why this happened.

For example, during the pandemic the numbers of people downloading Zoom increased dramatically, resulting in '31,100 new customers, or 61% year-over-year' (Zoom, 2020, p. 2). In this situation, we can analyse the data and the insights are clear: it was due to the urgent need to work from home, home-schooling and general communications. This is not a typical situation and if this had happened in a 'typical year' we would need to investigate why, which may involve using online surveys or interviews.

Which metrics should I use?

There are frequent questions about the types of metrics that should be used and evaluation depends on the measures you selected when creating the objectives. If you're struggling to see if a plan worked or not, it's because the metrics were weak. If this is the case, return to your objectives in STEP 4 and adjust where needed.

If you want to explore this step further, there is an entire chapter dedicated to digital marketing metrics and analytics in the textbook *Digital Marketing: Strategic Planning & Integration* by Annmarie Hanlon.

Notes:

_____

_____

_____

_____

_____

_____

_____

_____

7.5 Consider how you will evaluate your plan

Having considered **STEP 7** and the different options, how will you evaluate your plan?

What tools or techniques are needed?

Make your notes here:

You can find more space for notes in the Scribble Space at the back of the book!

Summary

You have considered how to evaluate your plan to see whether it worked and why. This demonstrated that some of the earlier objectives created for the case example of Zoom didn't work. They seemed specific and measurable, but when an evaluation was required, it was too difficult. This resulted in changing the earlier objectives.

Your plan is now complete. You have worked through the following steps:

STEP 1 - ASSESS THE BACKGROUND

STEP 2 - ANALYSE THE AUDIENCE

STEP 3 - CREATE A DIGITAL MARKETING STRATEGY

STEP 4- CONSTRUCT OBJECTIVES

STEP 5 - JUSTIFY THE RESOURCES

STEP 6 - BUILD THE ACTION PLAN

STEP 7 - EVALUATE THE PLAN

By working through each element, your plan is now ready to assemble and present to the senior management team.

Notes:

_____

_____

_____

_____

_____

_____

_____

_____

_____

STEP 8

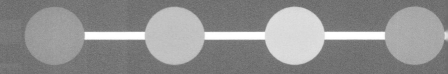

PRESENT
THE PLAN

Congratulations! If you are reading this page, you have created all the components for your plan and now it's time to share the work.

There are three main areas to consider in presenting a plan:

- What are the presentation options?

- What is the purpose of the plan?

- Who is the audience?

Let's explore each of these, but first it's useful for you to better understand your favourite learning style which may influence how you prefer to receive presentations.

Learning styles are recognised as being visual, aural, read/write and kinaesthetic (VARK), and the challenge is that your learning style might not be the same as that of your audience! Once you understand your style, you may also realise that this is why you are biased towards slides, lectures or videos.

8.1 Discover your learning style

Visit vark-learn.com to understand more about the different learning styles. The questionnaire is free to take and ranks the scores for your main preferences, which you can note here:

V

A

R

K

If you have some similar scores, this indicates a blended style. So you might like to read documents (R) with many images (V).

When you understand your learning style, you'll also realise that this may be the way you prefer to present information, but don't forget, the audience may have a different style.

Presentation options

Using the VARK systems, we know that many learners prefer imagery (visual), some like to listen to a presentation (aural), others prefer to review written material (read/write) and a smaller number prefer a hands-on practical experience (kinaesthetic).

You can see how social media has moved from the original Twitter posts – words only – to visual styles such as Instagram and a kinaesthetic approach using TikTok duets.

Using the VARK model, the presentation options include those shown in Table 8.1.

	Visual	Aural	Written	Kinaesthetic
Document	✓		✓	
Slides	✓	✓		✓
Podcast		✓		
Blog	✓		✓	
Video	✓	✓		
Infographic	✓			
Live presentation	✓	✓		✓

Table 8.1   Presentation styles based on the VARK model

The advantages and disadvantages of these presentation options depend on many factors such as:

- The amount of time available to complete the plan, considering your overall workload

- Your skill set in choosing one of these options, if you are the person that needs to prepare the material

8.2 Evaluate the presentation options

Consider the advantages and disadvantages of these different presentation options and add to this table.

	Advantages	Disadvantages
Document		
Slides		
Podcast		
Blog		
Video		
Infographic		
Live presentation		

However, regardless of your skill set – as you can always improve or enhance your skills – it's important to be aware of best practice, which is shown in Table 8.2.

Presentation option	Best practice
Document	Written documents should be well-presented, spell-checked and include a contents page and page numbers. The text should be in an easy-to-read font with sufficient space around the lines for better readability.
Slides	Less is more! Some presenters suggest 10–20–30 which is a maximum of 10 slides, a presentation of no more than 20 minutes and a font size at a minimum of 30.
Podcast	To record a good podcast, you need to write a script and rehearse in advance.
Blog	Preparing a blog article needs advance planning to consider the heading (title) and sub-titles to keep the reader until the end of the page. Some imagery may be used to break up the text.
Video	A video can include you as the presenter or can be an animated story. This requires a good script, as well as good sound and lighting.
Infographic	Successful infographics tell a story with a beginning, middle and ending. They should be simple and avoid over-use of colour, sticking to a simple palette.
Live presentation	Live presentations require a great deal of practice and often learning the script in advance.

Table 8.2   Best practice for presentation options

8.3 Improve your presentation skills

Search online for 'best way to present a...' and select your preferred option to gain more guidance as to the best and poor practice for your preferred presentation style.

Add your notes here:

You can find more space for notes in the Scribble Space at the back of the book!

Purpose of the plan and the audience

Having explored the different options available, let's consider why you've created this digital marketing plan and who the intended audience may be, as shown in Figure 8.1.

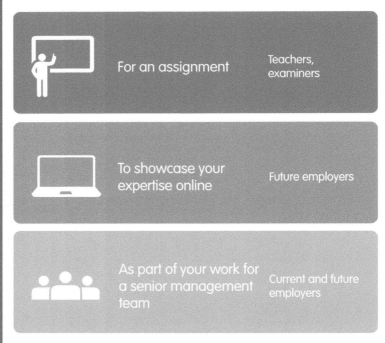

Figure 8.1 Purpose of the plan and the audience

Each of these purposes requires a different approach that's covered in this section.

For an assignment

The aim of the assignment is to pass a module. Your grade will depend on how closely you follow the instructions.

For example, an assignment usually states how many words or pages are permitted and the normal convention is to present the work as a report in a document. Table 8.3 shows the structure and key content needed when presenting a digital marketing plan for an assignment.

STEP	Key content
STEP 1 – ASSESS THE BACKGROUND	Two-page summary
STEP 2 – ANALYSE THE AUDIENCE	Two personas on two pages
STEP 3 – CREATE A DIGITAL MARKETING STRATEGY	Strategy statement summarized in a paragraph
STEP 4 – CONSTRUCT OBJECTIVES	Objectives linked to strategy in a table with an explainer paragraph
STEP 5 – JUSTIFY THE RESOURCES	Resources relating to objectives, stated in a paragraph with a summary budget
STEP 6 – BUILD THE ACTION PLAN	Gantt chart or online tool showing the plan
STEP 7 – EVALUATE THE PLAN	Table showing how the objectives will be evaluated

Table 8.3 Presenting a digital marketing plan for an assignment

To showcase your expertise online

To showcase your expertise online, instead of presenting a document, you might extract the key points from each part and present the digital marketing plan as an infographic with summary headings, as shown in Figure 8.2.

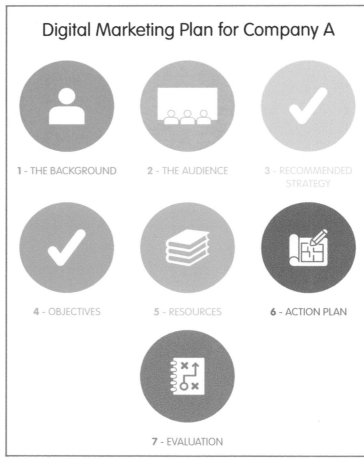

Figure 8.2 Digital marketing plan infographic

Other options include setting up a free blog account on wordpress. com or medium.com and using this as a wider portfolio to showcase more of your work.

As part of your work for a senior management team

If this is a work project and you're expecting to present to a wider group of people, such as a senior management team, you need to take a slightly different approach.

The company already knows the background, so it can be better to prepare a formal Word document for those that prefer this – you've already done most of this – and to summarise key points on a slide deck. All you need are nine slides, as shown in Table 8.4.

STEP	Key content
STEP 1 – THE BACKGROUND	Summary on two slides
STEP 2 – THE AUDIENCE	Two personas on two slides
STEP 3 – RECOMMENDED DIGITAL MARKETING STRATEGY	Strategy statement summarised in a paragraph on one slide
STEP 4 – OBJECTIVES	Objectives linked to strategy in a table with an explainer paragraph
STEP 5 – RESOURCES	Resources relating to objectives, in a table on one slide A summary budget on another slide
STEP 6 – BUILD THE ACTION PLAN	Gantt chart or similar showing actions needed
STEP 7 – EVALUATE THE PLAN	Table showing how the objectives will be evaluated on a slide

Table 8.4   Presenting a digital marketing plan for work

Having considered the best ways to present a plan, let's explore the Zoom plan and examine how this could be presented.

Let's imagine the plan is being presented to the newly appointed group marketing lead. They're a busy person leading a global team. Using the power/interest matrix from **STEP 6**, it's clear that the group marketing lead has a high level of interest in the plan and if I'm reporting to this person, they have a high level of power too, so the guidelines are to 'manage closely' and ensure they are kept informed of all the details. First, I'll assess what's needed, then I'll create the presentation.

STEP 1 – ASSESS THE BACKGROUND

Zoom will be aware of the impact of the 7Ps within the micro-environment as well as the PESTLE factors in the macro-environment, so it wouldn't be relevant to repeat those details. This information could be added as appendices to a written document. Additional information that may be useful in the presentation, such as the 7Cs applied to Zoom, could be displayed as an edited table on a slide.

STEP 2 – ANALYSE THE AUDIENCE

In this example, I'll present just one of the personas and I'll select the B2B persona as this is where the focus of the growth strategy lies. This will be presented on a slide, with images to make it more realistic.

STEP 3 – CREATE A DIGITAL MARKETING STRATEGY

A summary of the strategy will be presented on one slide with the different elements numbered, but clearly marked as a growth strategy.

STEP 4 – CONSTRUCT THE OBJECTIVES

The objectives will be summarised on one slide and I'll take out the ones that don't work (those focusing on 'launches' in countries). I can always mention this in a discussion.

STEP 5 – JUSTIFY THE RESOURCES

Rather than explain all the resources needed, I'll summarise the budget on one slide.

Having figured out what's needed and because I want to impress my new boss, I will:

- Prepare a slide presentation

- Practice how I will deliver this to an audience, including other team members

- Add my earlier content to a document, with appendices at the back to support my arguments

Figure 8.3 shows an example of how the presentation might look. This meets the first part of the 10–20–30 rule as it's fewer than 10 slides.

Annmarie's Advice

When creating any form of presentation, make sure you understand the purpose of the work and the audience!

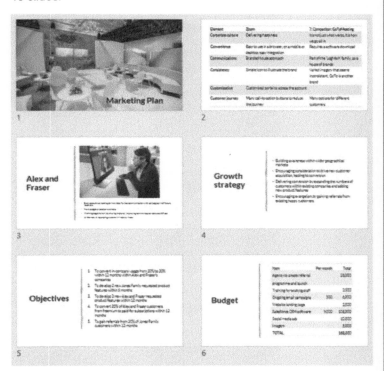

Figure 8.3 Example presentation of the Zoom action plan

8.4 Finalise how you will present your digital marketing plan

Having considered **STEP 8** and the different options, how will you deliver your presentation? Add notes at the end of this step or in the Scribble Space at the back of the book!

Make your notes here:

You can find more space for notes in the Scribble Space at the back of the book!

Summary

Well done! You've reached the final stage and have created a digital marketing plan that you're ready to present, whether that's:

- For an assignment
- To showcase your work online
- As part of your work within a company

You have now learned the skills involved in creating a digital marketing plan and have:

1. Assessed the organisation's background
2. Analysed the audience and created personas
3. Created a digital marketing strategy
4. Constructed strong and SMART objectives
5. Justified the resources and presented a summary budget
6. Constructed the action plan
7. Evaluated the plan to ensure it will work
8. Prepared to present the plan

Don't forget to create a summary of your achievements and add this to your CV and online professional social media pages like LinkedIn.

Checklist

1.1	Create your customer journey	☐
1.2	Choose a company for your case example	☐
1.3	Develop the organisation background	☐
1.4	Apply the 7Ps	☐
1.5	Assess the macro-environment of your organisation	☐
1.6	Outline the strengths and weaknesses of the main competitors	☐
1.7	Apply the 7Cs	☐
2.1	Explore persona tools	☐
2.2	Search online for more on your chosen company	☐
2.3	Ask the librarian!	☐
2.4	Examine the social media spaces	☐
2.5	Assess the data that's available to you	☐
2.6	Find free images	☐
2.7	Find the keywords	☐
2.8	Create a persona for your organisation	☐
3.1	The lost companies	☐
3.2	Check the PESTLE details	☐
3.3	New company discovery	☐
3.4	Your strategic options	☐
3.5	Take the strategy to the next level	☐
3.6	Your strategy statement	☐
4.1	Create an objective	☐
4.2	Review your objective	☐
4.3	Refine your objective	☐
4.4	Try the Google Analytics Demo account	☐
4.5	Find the weak or strong objectives	☐
4.6	Create 3 SMART objectives for your company	☐

5.1	Explore job roles	☐
5.2	Explore company budgets	☐
5.3	The cost of outsourcing	☐
5.4	The impact of Mother Nature	☐
5.5	Your measurement tool	☐
5.6	Explore costs of email software systems	☐
5.7	The cost of materials	☐
5.8	Identify your management supporter	☐
5.9	Estimate the time needed	☐
5.10	Identify the required resources for 2 of your company's objectives	☐
5.11	Outline the budget	☐
6.1	Create a stakeholder map	☐
6.2	Develop a power / interest matrix	☐
6.3	Create a Gantt chart for two of your objectives	☐
6.4	Search online for free project management tools	☐
7.1	Suggest the benchmarks	☐
7.2	Search for survey tools	☐
7.3	Review two of your objectives to demonstrate evaluation	☐
7.4	Check your analytics	☐
7.5	How will you evaluate your plan?	☐
8.1	What's your learning style?	☐
8.2	Evaluate the presentation options	☐
8.3	Improve your presentation skills	☐
8.4	How will you present your digital marketing plan?	☐

References

Ansoff, H.I. (1957) 'Strategies for diversification', *Harvard Business Review*, September, pp. 113–24.

Booms, B.H. and Bitner, M.J. (1980) 'New management tools for the successful tourism manager', *Annals of Tourism Research*, 7 (3), pp. 337–52.

Chartered Institute of Marketing (2009) 'Marketing and the 7Ps: What is marketing? A brief summary of marketing and how it works'. Maidenhead, Berkshire: Chartered Institute of Marketing, p. 10. Available at: www.cim. co.uk/marketingresources (accessed 18 October 2014).

Dommett, K. (2019) 'The rise of online political advertising', *Political Insight*, *10* (4), pp. 12–15. doi: 10.1177/2041905819891366.

Freeman, R.E.E. and McVea, J. (2005) 'A stakeholder approach to strategic management', in *Handbook of Strategic Management*. Oxford: Blackwell, pp. 189–207.

Gantt, H.L. (1919) *Organizing for Work*. New York: Harcourt, Brace and Howe Inc.

Gay, R., Charlesworth, A. and Esen, R. (2007) *Online Marketing: A Customer-led Approach*. Oxford: Oxford University Press.

Hanlon, A. (2022) *Digital Marketing: Strategic Planning & Integration*, 2nd edn. London: Sage.

Join WhatsApp (2021) Scams Project Manager. Available at: www.whatsapp. com/join/?dept=whatsapp&id=a1K2K000007oZYwUAM (accessed 25 January 2021).

Kozinets, R.V. (2002) 'The field behind the screen: Using netnography for marketing research in online communities', *Journal of Marketing Research*, *39* (1), pp. 61–72. Available at: http://journals.ama.org/doi/abs/10.1509/ jmkr.39.1.61.18935.

Management Systems Corporation (1961) *An Introduction to the PERT/Cost System: For Integrated Project Management*. Washington, DC. Available at: https://hdl.handle.net/2027/uc1.d0002535581.

Mäntymäki, M., Islam, A.K.M.N. and Benbasat, I. (2020) 'What drives subscribing to premium in freemium services? A consumer value-based view of differences between upgrading to and staying with premium', *Information Systems Journal*, *30* (2), pp. 295–333. doi: 10.1111/isj.12262.

Mendelow, A.L. (1981) 'Environmental scanning: The impact of the stakeholder concept', Proceedings of the International Conference on Information Systems, pp. 407–17.

Zoom (2020) Annual Report. San Jose, CA. Available at: https://investors. zoom.us/static-files/28614884-1d63-477a-9148-a7039796f19c.

Zoom Careers (2021) Sr. Security Analyst. Available at: https://zoom.wd5. myworkdayjobs.com/en-US/Zoom/job/Denver-CO/Sr-Security-Analyst-- SOC_R994-1 (accessed 25 January 2021).

*Scribble space
for your ideas*

Here's some extra space for you to make notes